Guidance 24/7

How to Open Your Heart
and Let Angels Into Your Life

Christel Nani, RN, Medical Intuitive

L.M. Press
Cayucos, California

Copyright © 2005 by Christel Nani
First printing, 2005
Second printing, 2006

Cataloguing-in-Publication Data
Nani, Christel
    Guidance 24/7: How to Open Your Heart and
    Let Angels Into Your Life / Christel Nani. – 1st ed.
    p. cm.

 ISBN: 0-9741450-3-3

Other books by Christel Nani:

Diary of a Medical Intuitive: One Woman's Eye-Opening Journey from No-Nonsense E.R. Nurse to Open-Hearted Healer and Visionary

Sacred Choices: Thinking Outside the Tribe to Heal Your Spirit, Harmony Books, October 2006

CR

DEDICATION

To my Mom & Dad
for teaching me the importance of integrity,
forgiveness, and compassion, and for making me
the person I am today.

ACKNOWLEDGEMENTS

My profound gratitude to God,
all the angels, and St. Jude for always being there,
and for the gift of Grace. Thank you to my editor,
Margot Silk Forrest, cover designer Peri Poloni, and
to all of my clients who are smart enough and
courageous enough to ask for
help.

ABOUT THE AUTHOR

The Rev. Christel Nani, RN, is a gifted Medical Intuitive who uses her clairvoyant vision to read a person's energetic blueprint with pinpoint accuracy, locating the unconscious traumas, decisions and emotional patterns contributing to a patient's physical, emotional and spiritual illness. Her talent for identifying the one priority task that will reverse these patterns is a true channeling of spiritual goodness.

Nani, an Interfaith minister, is the founder of the Center for Spiritual Responsibility in Encinitas, CA.

She can be reached via her website, www.christelnani.com, or email info@christelnani.com.

Table of Contents

Guidance 24/7

Foreword

By Rebecca Grace, Psy.D.

You have been guided to this book. You may not know why, but something inside you is telling you to read it. Now you have a choice: to follow your guidance or to ignore the quiet longing of your heart. The choice you make will put into motion energies that can bring your life into flow, or leave it stuck in struggle. And your choice is determined by powerful unconscious beliefs that have always stood between you and a full relationship with God.

Knowing you are never alone, are always loved and always protected will change your life forever. It will not eliminate bumps in the road, but it will shelter you from feeling lonely, afraid, or deeply uncertain about what to do.

This book is written by a woman who knows God and helps others to discover the spirit of love for themselves. She does not preach a religion or prescribe a path. She simply reads people's souls and tells them how they are blocking their connection to God. She changes their lives by healing their spirits.

I know her work intimately because she read my soul and told me what I needed to change in order to know God's love for me. It did not require a trip to India, fasting, taking a vow of poverty or renouncing my lifestyle. I did not have to sacrifice or give up anything important to me. I did not have to carefully watch my thoughts, obsessively allowing only the "positive" ones in. I did not have to suffer, pay a price, or jump through hoops. I did, however, have to give up all my beliefs that God required payment for any goodness in my life.

Most of us know *in our heads* that God loves us unconditionally. Some people, however, don't even know that. I was once one of them. A rigid, scary, fundamentalist upbringing can stamp out any positive feelings toward God. So can childhood abuse and a hundred other things that can go wrong.

But to know in your heart – deep, deep down – that you are loved and cherished, that's a very different experience. It's one that is fully available. Imagine being able to discover that block inside you that keeps you from accepting the full presence of God's unconditional love into your life. Then imagine being able to change it. And imagine the change is quick and easy.

This book can bring you to God. It's not so hard; we just tend to think it is. All that's required is an open mind. Open yourself to the possibility that you carry some damaging beliefs that are hurting you and causing a huge amount of unnecessary pain in your life. Open your mind to the possibility that changing those beliefs changes everything.

Rebecca Grace
Encinitas, California
November 14, 2004

CHAPTER 1

Your Biggest Problem, Easily Solved

I read souls for a living, and I know a person's deepest secrets. I have been clairvoyant since age eight and am now a medical intuitive and healer. During an intuitive reading, I see a running "video" of your childhood at lightning speed. This video reveals the traumas you have endured, your personal beliefs about yourself, your level of self-esteem, and more. I also see your secrets.

*   *   *

One of the most common secrets I find is that people are afraid to ask for help because they don't think they deserve it. Over and over, I see how a person's reluctance to ask for help creates a multitude of problems in their lives. These problems are *self-created*. They aren't inevitable. They aren't inherited.

They aren't fate. Frequently people defend their difficulties as "just a part of life," but I know that is not true.

They aren't even "just the way things are." I know your life does not have to be filled with difficulties – even if other people's lives are.

During an intuitive reading, when I look deeper into your past, I learn the many rational reasons you have for refusing to ask for help. These include thinking you are not good enough because you had an abortion, for example, or left a marriage. Sometimes you take great pride in struggling with your problems and overcoming adversity on your own. You believe that it builds character.

You might have given up asking for help because you thought you never got a response, or you got an answer you didn't like, or you got guidance that flew in the face of all that was logical – like being told to leave a good job that you adored for an uncertain future. (That's exactly what happened to me when I was guided to give up my successful career as a trauma and E.R. nurse and make my living full-time as a medical intuitive. No benefits package, job security, or pension plan there!) Maybe you have too much pride to admit you need help, or maybe are just afraid to ask for it.

If any of these reasons ring true for you, read on.

I can show you how to *easily* remove these barriers to getting the guidance you need and deserve. If you feel skeptical when you hear me say "easily," we'll talk about that too. For now, just ask yourself: Why am I objecting to something important being easy to do?

There is one other reason you might not ask for God's help, and it is this: You want to handle your problems on your own. If you are proud of your ability to overcome adversity single-handed, be forewarned. If you keep reading, this book will shake your world to its foundations.

When I see people struggling through life, I know it doesn't need to be this way. There is no good reason not to ask for and receive God's help. It's like not asking for directions and driving around lost for days and days. If you're on your way to visit a new friend, it's just silly. If you're on your way to the emergency room, it's tragic.

I have to tell you that your objections to seeking help are all manmade. In other words, you made them up. (Or someone else made them up and convinced you they were true.) In God's eyes, there is no reason not to ask for help.

God will help you each and every time you ask. You may not recognize the help you are sent – we'll talk about this more later – but it will always arrive, and you can learn to recognize it. Spiritual helpers, guides, and angels are available to every one of us no matter what we've done in the past, no matter what our situation is in the present. Whether the help you need is an answer to a straightforward question, a solution to a serious problem, guidance about your next step in life, or something as simple as how to find North Maple Street, you can get it just for the asking.

There is nothing standing between you and a wealth of assistance. Nothing, that is, except your own lack of willingness, some erroneous cultural and personal beliefs, and your pride. Maybe these things seem too big or too hard to change. Maybe they seem like they would require long-term therapy or extensive inner-growth work. They won't.

Overcoming them requires only one thing: being willing to consider the possibility that you are wrong, that you have been in the throes of stinking thinking when it comes to receiving help from God. In this book I will show you how to get into "right thinking." *Easily.* If you think change of this magnitude can't come easily, that it has to be hard work, that's just an erroneous cultural belief. I call these kinds of beliefs "tribal beliefs" and you can change them...easily. I'll show you how in Chapter 10.

Some of you may recognize the wonderful term

"stinking thinking"
from Alcoholics
Anonymous. It refers
to a whole range of
negative thinking
that warps our
relationships with
ourselves and others.
When you are
submerged in
stinking thinking,
nothing will change
until you are willing
to open up to the
possibility that your
thinking could be

Openness

Please help me let go
of any rigid "black-and-
white" thinking and be
open to new ideas that
can change my life for the
better. Help me to listen
with my heart, not my
mind.

wrong, that it might even be source of your discomfort.

Yes, I know you have invested a lot of time and energy in believing you don't deserve help, and I know you don't like being wrong, but if you could set those concepts aside momentarily, I have a surprise for you. Life doesn't have to be as hard as you are making it. What's more, you will receive no brownie points either here or in the sweet hereafter for your fortitude in overcoming adversity. The badge of honor you wear so proudly doesn't go with you when you cross over.

I have been privileged to accompany a number of people on their journey to the afterlife, and I can tell you from my firsthand knowledge that there is no special section for those who have managed to get through life without any help. There's only one big "room" up there and everyone is bathed alike in the softest light. It is the most loving and safe place you will ever know. There is no struggle, pain, or disease. There is only unconditional love, joy, and the freedom to be loved. It is here that angels and spiritual helpers wait to help you. The good news is that you don't need to wait for your death to see or feel the presence of these spiritual helpers.

Angels, as I like to call them, are available to you anytime you ask. How do I know this? Because every time I have convinced someone to ask for help, he or she has received it – and that includes the sinners, the good people, the nonbelievers, and the faithful alike.

Whenever I ask God for help, I receive it generally within 48 hours, if not a lot sooner. It comes in the form of an answer or a solution to a perplexing problem, a lifting of my spirit during times of sadness or grief, or direct guidance on what I should do next. And with it always comes the solace of knowing that I am not going through life alone.

I wrote this book to inspire you to change your ideas about asking for God's help and thus live an easier and more fulfilling life. I see so much needless struggle and suffering in this world, and as a medical intuitive, I know the harm it wreaks. I can literally see the ravages of these struggles on your heart, body, and mind – and eventually on your soul.

When I do an intuitive reading, I look at the amount of light emanating from your soul. I also look at your past and see your soul when you were a child, before you got hurt, learned to believe bad things about yourself, or learned that struggling builds character. I see you before you began taking pride in your struggle. Your child soul thrums with vitality and love and light.

Then I see the progressive darkening of your spirit. Your pride, ego, shadow – whatever you want to call it, it's all the same – dims the beautiful light of your soul and separates you from God. Beliefs like *I don't deserve any help from God* or *I can handle this on my own* swarm over your soul like a dark gray shadow, trying to suffocate it.

But even the biggest and darkest shadows will still show pinpricks of light coming through. So when I read your soul in present time, I can glimpse the essence of who you really are and the amazing YOU that you have a choice to become.

This book is to guide you to become that person. If you want to follow that path easily, I suggest you set your intention by saying the prayers in the little boxes as we go along. Setting your intention, praying, asking for help from a spiritual guide, or simply choosing to be in a state of openness is a great beginning. Remember, it's your brain that decided to be rigid about its beliefs, not your soul.

Let me tell you more about your soul. Since the soul is not of this world, it is without ego or pride. It is who you really are, and seeing the true you is always an awe-inspiring experience for me. Remember that light-filled heavenly "room"? Each time I do a reading, I see a glimpse of that same light in your soul. That glimpse fills me with joy and inner peace.

This first glimpse of your light is familiar, loving, and exciting to me. But just as my view of that "room" gradually fades from me as I fall back to earth and return to physical form, my first glimpse of your shining soul fades from my view. It is replaced by the sight of the shadowy film now covering your soul. The joy and love that were once so bright have been replaced by judgment, fear, anger, and low-self esteem.

It makes me long to see you uncover your soul, strip away the shadowy film and free your light to shine. Uncovering his soul enabled a great musician (who had truly believed he wasn't good enough) to reach the top of the charts. It has allowed people to heal from incurable diseases and has brought an inner peace to those suffering from tremendous feelings of inadequacy. It has healed victims of abuse and given courage to those who lived in fear.

Your soul is directly connected to God. It is the part of you that recognizes truth, burns with inspiration and kindness, revels in forgiveness and compassion, and yearns to love unconditionally. It is the part of you that is most like God. But your life experiences can dim your soul and separate you from God. When you learn prejudice or harbor vengeance, for example, a shadow falls across your soul. The choices you make as an adult – including the refusal to ask for help or open up to a new way of thinking – play a major role in dimming the light of your soul.

In only a very few instances have I seen a person so removed from his true essence that his soul has been completely blotted out by the darkness. One of

---

Peace of Mind

Please help me quiet my mind of any objections or fears that stand in the way of my exploring a new way of living.

the times I did see this, the darkness was created by the man's own choices. He was someone who had to be right even though it hurt him and others. He was in the throes of stinking thinking. He refused to take responsibility for the life he had created for himself and blamed others for his woes.

This unwillingness and rigidity take tremendous effort. You must work diligently to keep proving how right you are, and you must be vigilant in your refusal to explore a different paradigm from the one you now so dearly cling to. You must hold onto your belief that you are bad or deserve to be punished, or that help is not available to you because you are flawed and therefore different from those who are able to receive help.

Can you open up to the possibility that help is available to you here and now *if you were to only ask?* Or do you prefer to be "special?"

The answer to your biggest problem – your separation from God – is here in this book. I can help you tear away the shadowy film over your soul that keeps you powerless and unhappy and maybe even ill. I will show you how your soul can illuminate this world by being who it really is, not what you and others have forced it to become.

But I can only do this if you are willing.

I want you, right here and right now, to say

you'll give it a try. No excuses. It won't cost you a thing. All you have to lose is the biggest problem in your life. And I know how much you have to gain – it's written in light across your soul.

CHAPTER 2

What's Stopping You?

Asking for guidance begins with opening – and staying open – to the possibility that your old way of thinking is not correct. Are you willing to consider that everyone who asks for God's help – including you – will get it? Are you also willing to consider that this help is not earned or bought, that it is a form of grace? Put simply, grace is help from God that we receive just because we asked for it.

*　　　*　　　*

It's important for you to know that none of the things I am telling you come from the tenets of any particular religion. What I know about God and how God's love works is based on my actual experience. Because I have traveled to the other side and seen angels and spiritual helpers, I know they exist. I know they will come whenever you ask for help and are with you when you die. This is fact, whether you choose to believe it or not.

For anyone who wants to argue or debate the truth of these statements, I would ask: "Why do you want to work so hard to disprove something so good?" You have a choice where you invest your energy. Does it make sense to waste it on debate or excuses instead of simply trying out the truth of what I'm saying?

If you can't get past your need to disprove the reality of angels, spiritual helpers, and divine guidance, please skip to Chapter 11. That's where I'll talk about your pride and your ego, which are the only things standing in the way of your life becoming infinitely less complicated and a heck of a lot more fun.

Let's return to the irrefutable fact that divine guidance is always available and all you have to do is ask for it. Answer me this: do you ask for God's help when your life isn't going well? Do you ask for help when you need an answer to a question? Do you ask for help when you are depressed or sad, or feel like you are bending under the weight of your life? Probably not.

Now imagine you are stuck in quicksand and are slowly sinking beneath the surface. Would you ask for help? Of course you would. You know that if you don't, you will sink deeper and deeper until you suffocate and die. I bet you'd shout for help at the top of your lungs!

But what if I told you that you were sinking closer and closer to suffocation every time you refuse to ask for God's help? Without help, you are expending needless energy struggling to overcome the problems in your life. And just like struggling to get out of quicksand, all that happens is you use up your energy, sink even faster, and eventually lose the battle anyway.

What I am trying to tell you is that the quality of your life is on the line – you can choose to make your life painful and difficult, or joyous and flowing. You can choose to live with guidance, or you can choose to die without it. I am not exaggerating.

When I used the analogy of the quicksand, it was easy for you to see the seriousness of the situation: if you think you will die, you won't hesitate to ask for help. But asking for God's help becomes more complicated if you don't recognize you are dying. Subtle, life-draining (as opposed to life-threatening) situations arise all the time in your life. And because you don't realize the real danger in tolerating such situations, you put off asking for help, or you debate whether you ought to ask, or you take time to worry whether you deserve it.

This debating costs you dearly. The high price you are paying for it is clear to me when I do a reading of your soul. I can see exactly how your choice to struggle through life without God's help is draining your energy, affecting your daily health and happiness, and wreaking long-term damage on your physical, emotional, and spiritual well-being.

Let's try a different analogy, one that I often use with my clients. We have established that if your life were at stake, you would have no hesitation asking for help. What about when your emotional life is at stake, like when you feel deeply hurt, lonely, or depressed? It's not immediately life-threatening like being stuck in quicksand. It's more like twisting your ankle deep within a forest just as the sun is going down. It's probably not going to kill you, and you can certainly tolerate the discomfort.

Is it easy for you to ask for help in this kind of situation? Pretend that as you are lying there with your ankle swelling up. You see a stranger hiking a little way away. She

✧

Compassion

Please help me be compassionate with myself and others as I examine some of the choices I have made in my life.

doesn't see you. Would you call out and ask her to go for help? What if you were hiking with a friend? Would you ask him to help carry you out of the woods even though night is already falling and the journey could take a couple of hours? What if a big old St. Bernard lollopped up? Would you pet her and get her to stay with you during the long hours when the tranquil forest was transformed into a dark, frightening, and maybe dangerous place?

Why are you thinking so much? Why even consider tolerating an uncomfortable night in the woods when you could simply shout, "I need some help!" Because your pesky thoughts are standing in your way. Maybe you think you are weak because you can't limp or hop your way out of the forest on your own. Maybe you think you shouldn't ask other people to go out of their way to help you.

Isn't it amazing how your thoughts and beliefs can complicate a very simple situation? Here you are debating with yourself about what's acceptable to ask from a stranger and what's acceptable to ask from a friend while the sun is setting and the temperature's dropping. You could end up spending the night in the forest freezing your butt off just because your thoughts kept you from getting the help you needed.

So, setting aside our second analogy, when your

emotional life is at risk, what stops you asking for help from God or your Higher Power? (Whether you think of God as a friend or a stranger doesn't matter because God doesn't care. You'll receive help either way.) When I ask my clients why they don't ask for help, I hear the same reasons over and over:

- "I don't deserve help."
- "My problems are small, and it's not right to ask for help when there are people worse off than me, people who really need the help."
- "Asking for help means I'm weak."
- "If I ask for help and get it, I will owe something, and I don't like the feeling of owing something."
- "I didn't know I could ask for help."
- "Asking for help means losing my independence."
- "If I struggle through on my own, it builds character."
- "Asking for help is embarrassing. It implies I'm a failure."
- "Asking for help means letting go of control."
- "It's not right to bother people with my problems."

- "I thought only spiritual or good people received help."
- "I don't know how to ask for help."
- "God never answers my prayers."

If you identified with any of the above reasons, I'm here to tell you that your ideas are pure unadulterated crap. They all come from your stinking thinking. There is an error in your logic and in the conclusions you have drawn.

You are the one who has decided that a friend or stranger will judge you as weak if you ask for help. (Maybe they'd actually think you were smart. Asking for something when you need it is smart.) You are the one who has decided that you will owe something in return. You are the one who is puzzling over whether you deserve help or not. That dog certainly isn't – and neither is God. And you are the one who assumes you will always recognize divine help when you receive it.

The only thing that's getting in the way of asking for help is your attitude. Are you so attached to your conclusions and your beliefs that you would suffer for the right not to change or examine them? Would you rather be right and freeze your butt off in the forest or open up to the possibility that your thinking is in error? If you'd rather be right, close this book and get your money back. It's not for you.

I always find it interesting that none of the many objections to asking for help applies when it comes to the St. Bernard. You would have no hesitation in keeping the dog with you in the forest. Were she able to drag you

Courage

Please help me display my courage by choosing to make something else – like being of service to others – more important than my fear of asking God for help.

back to civilization, you wouldn't hesitate to ask her. Why is that? First of all, that's what St. Bernards do. It's their purpose in life: They help people. Second, dogs never judge you or expect anything in return. Third, dogs love you unconditionally. They are excited to see you, thrilled to be with you, and eager to help you. Knowing those things makes all the difference.

I am telling you for a fact that the same unconditional love is surrounding you right now. It's so close, it could lick your face. Think of it as a legion of St. Bernards just waiting for the chance to come to your rescue. Angels, spiritual guides, and other divine helpers exist in order to come to your aid. They never judge you, and they never expect anything in return.

The help they bring is divine guidance. And it's available 24/7.

Just open your heart and ask.

CHAPTER 3

How to Recognize Divine Guidance When You Get It

Although divine guidance is available 24/7, it is not called on as frequently as you would think. Often that's because people are not sure if what they hear is really divine guidance or just their own thoughts. Divine guidance can come to you as a gentle whisper or a booming voice, an inner knowing, a profound dream, or a visit from an angel. Most often it will come in the form of an intuition or inspiration. An intuition is a sudden knowing that comes without logic, thought, or effort. It is when you simply know something is true or right. An inspiration, on the other hand, is a revelation, an idea that's quite outside of your normal way of thinking. It is creative – it pulls you up and out of your old ways. Like intuition, inspiration comes from God – think of Michelangelo or Beethoven or the moment you realized that your life *didn't have to be as hard as you were making it. By the end of this section, you'll know how to discern divine guidance from your own thoughts.*

*　　　*　　　*

All you need to do to ask for divine guidance is to pray. Talk to God, your Higher Power, angels, or spiritual helpers and ask for help in making a decision, guidance on what to do next, comfort from your despair, or whatever else you need help with. Sometimes your request will be specific, such as "Should I take this job?" Other times you simply feel stuck or lost. Whether you pray for specific help or general guidance, you will receive what's best for you. God knows what you need.

How long before you hear back? It could literally take seconds, or it could take a bit longer. I have never gone more than 48 hours without an answer – unless I did not really want an answer out of fear that I wouldn't like it. Imagine praying for guidance about your relationship, but being afraid that you will learn you must leave it? Are you truly putting your heart and soul into your request for an answer? This is a vital aspect to hearing your guidance and I'll explain more about it in a moment.

If your prayer for guidance is wholehearted but you haven't heard back in a few days, listen carefully. Pay close attention to your dreams, to the people you come in contact with – who may be angels in disguise – and to "coincidences" that crop up. (Personally, I don't believe in coincidences – I think it's God trying to get our attention.) Guidance can come in all these forms.

Honesty

Please help me speak my truth and communicate clearly when I ask for guidance, and become aware of any reasons I have for not wanting an answer.

Most often, though, it comes in the form of an inner knowing. Sometimes you will hear a soft, clear voice in your head, as I did when God told me to leave my beloved work in the E.R. and use my intuitive gifts full-time. There was no thinking involved on my part, no decision to make, no inner debate about should I or shouldn't I do this. I didn't like the message, but it came nonetheless with a feeling of complete knowing.

You can recognize guidance because it's simple, clear, and direct. It is an idea that comes to you without any thought, discussion, debate, or supporting evidence that it is the right thing to do. Also, guidance arrives with no emotional charge attached to it – that comes later. All you feel in the instant that guidance arrives is gratitude for the idea or the answer you have been given.

However, when we start thinking about our guidance and we decide we don't like it and will ignore it, the soft voice often changes into a powerful and booming command that sounds like someone is yelling into your ear with a megaphone: "LEAVE THE E.R. AND USE YOUR GIFTS FULL-TIME!"

Whether you hear the soft or the booming voice, you will know it is genuine guidance because what it says will run through you in a way that feels true – truth always resonates inside you. Just as when you reach a conclusion about an issue and you know it is correct, guidance runs through your body in a way that tells you that you have discovered a truth. When you feel this happening, you are in alignment with your soul.

Guidance always feels this way in the moment it comes to you. If you don't like your guidance, you will debate it or fight it or come up with a multitude of excuses why it isn't the best thing for you. But that doesn't change the guidance. Guidance is truth, and truth cannot be negotiated. For example, you can't negotiate the truth that harming others is wrong.

You can't convince yourself otherwise and remain in alignment with your soul. This is the best definition of truth: that which is in alignment with your soul, the part of you most like God.

Truth is an idea that "feels right" or an inspiration that burns within you because it comes from your Higher Power or God. Guidance comes from a place of goodness and not ego, whether it is something simple like; "This is not the apartment for you," or something more dramatic such as "It's time to leave your marriage." Guidance puts your soul and heart at ease. It will never appeal to your brain or say, "You should do this because…"

While divine guidance can come as a whisper, a voice, a dream, a surprising stranger who crosses your path, an idea, a knowing, a nudge to do something, a coincidence, or a feeling, one aspect will always be the same: hearing it will always make you feel good, even when you don't like what you are being told. In that initial

✧

Guidance

Please help me ask for guidance from my Higher Power or God whenever I need to, not just when there is a large rut in my road of life.

moment of recognizing your guidance, a relief, a joy, an excitement runs through your whole being – until your darn brain thinks it over, sees how it will change your life, and hollers, "Are you crazy? No way!"

During one of my workshops a lovely man who was a social worker received guidance that it was time to change careers. Deep down, he felt relieved because he wouldn't have to listen to people's problems any more. His soul and heart were greatly eased until his brain demanded, "How will you support yourself?" That's when his fear kicked in. And when fear kicks in, your rational mind comes up with every logical, rational, and defensive reason to not follow the guidance you have been given.

You see, you won't always like your guidance even though it is always good for you. This bears repeating: Sometimes guidance sucks. It can appear to fly in the face of logic. Imagine you were told, as I was, to leave a wonderful job that you love, a secure job where you have risen on the ladder of success, a well-paying job, and set out in a virtually unknown field doing who knows what and who knows how? Wouldn't your brain shout, No way!

All the folks around me said as much at the time. Actually what they said was more like, "You are nuts, crazy, stupid! If you leave your job, what will you do, how will you do it, and how will you support yourself? What if you can't get another job as good as this one?" Naturally, I couldn't answer those questions because guidance doesn't always come with a detailed instruction book. We generally are given the goal or the first step toward that goal, but nothing more. What is demanded of us is radical trust.

But remember what I said about there being a feeling of truth when guidance comes? No matter how much I hated the guidance I was given to quit my nursing job, deep inside I could still feel it was the right thing for me to do.

When you are in this kind of situation, the only relevant question to ask yourself is, "How long will I debate my guidance and make myself miserable?" The social worker in my workshop had lasted almost eight years doing something he didn't like, and he was suffering from an incurable disease because his system had become so drained by his work. Hearing guidance to leave his job freed his soul and put him in alignment with his truth. Following his guidance is what he is working on now, but simply knowing his truth has brought his soul a sense of peace and freedom. He has stopped doing self-destructive things, takes better care of himself, and has begun to let people get closer to him. He also has started praying daily for himself and others. As to his "incurable" illness, it is almost gone. We expect he will soon get a full bill of health.

Bill, a musician, was also set free by following his guidance. He was a successful rock musician with a band but deep down wanted to play mellow acoustic guitar, and he wanted to play it solo. Of course, acoustic guitar solos are not as "cool" as rock music, so he struggled between wanting to keep his "cool" reputation and wanting to follow his heart's desire. Then his fear kicked in and he started thinking, "You were successful playing rock, so stick to what you know." How could he leave something he was good at to embark on an unknown course? He didn't know what to do. I told him to pray for guidance.

I mentioned earlier that one reason you may not hear your guidance is that you aren't open to hearing it. This is the reason that some prayers seem to go unanswered. Praying for guidance

> ### Trust
>
> Please help me choose to trust God's unconditional love for me and know that my highest good will always be revealed when I follow my guidance.

requires sincerity. You have to truly want an answer.
If not, you won't get one and you will think that God
is not answering your prayer, when the truth is that
you are not open to hearing the answer.

Part of being sincere in asking for guidance is
not putting conditions on the answer. It doesn't
work to pray, "Dear God, show me what to do but
don't make it be X or Y." I remember being plagued
by some painful physical symptoms and going for
tests to determine their cause. I already had done an
intuitive scan of myself and I knew what the diagnosis was, but I hadn't liked what I learned. I was hop-
ing for a different answer.

The lab ran my tests several times; sometimes
they came back positive, sometimes negative. My
doctors were baffled. I kept praying for a diagnosis
but heard nothing. This is strange, I thought. I've
never been without an answer to prayer. More
weeks of praying and still there was silence. Finally I
looked within myself to see if my prayer was sincere.
I had to face the fact that because I was ignoring the
diagnosis God showed me in the first place, my
prayer now for a diagnosis wasn't sincere.

I didn't actually want to know the truth; I
wanted a different "truth." Finally I decided that I
truly did want to know what was wrong with me,
and that night I prayed differently. I surrendered to

God's will, acknowledged my fear of hearing the truth, and trusted that God would be there for me. In other words, I took away the conditions I had set on the guidance I was asking for. Within a very short time, the lab was able to confirm a diagnosis of what was wrong – it was the same answer I had been given intuitively. But I had to genuinely want the answer, not just say I wanted it.

When you pray for guidance, you cannot attach conditions or rules such as, tell me this but not that. The bottom line is, don't pray for guidance until you want to hear the answer no matter what it is. If you are not ready to hear the answer, just pray for comfort, courage, and trust until you are ready.

When I asked Bill, the rock musician, if he was ready for whatever answer he received – whether it be to stick with the rock band or go into the unknown world of acoustic guitar – he agreed and prayed for divine guidance.

That night Bill had a dream: he was sitting in a doctor's office waiting when a doctor walked in and said, "If you continue to play rock music, you will go deaf," then walked out. End of dream. Bill didn't need me to interpret the dream. He gave up his connections to rock 'n' roll and began writing music more suited to solo guitar. And is he ever happy. I just heard that major doors are opening in his new career.

What's the secret to following guidance that seems to contradict common sense? What gave Bill the ability to walk away from his past success and status in the world of rock? It was his realization that when he had the dream, he felt the ring of truth resonate throughout his body. How did the social worker live down the sneers of his colleagues when he told them he was going to change careers and work with computers, which he'd always loved? He remembered how his heart had felt the moment he heard his guidance: relieved and very, very happy.

I guarantee you that following your guidance will always make your life better. How can you be sure? Look back to a moment in your life when you had that deep knowing and you chose to listen to it. Remember what it felt like. If you are truthful with yourself, it was probably a wonderful feeling that led to peace and calmness. Feel that calmness now and ask yourself, "After following my guidance, was my life better?"

For example, have you ever received guidance to leave a relationship and acted on it? Yes, doing so may have been painful and filled with duress, but look at the outcome, not the process. Did you heave a sigh of relief after making the decision to end your relationship?

When you fight your guidance by putting it off or pretending it isn't true, things become quite painful and distressing. When you listen and follow through, your life changes almost instantly.

I look at my life now, after listening to the completely illogical guidance to leave my beloved job in the ER. And guess what? Even though my life was pretty good then, it's a thousand times better now on all levels. As for all those fearful people who encouraged me not to do it, now they want to know where I got the courage and how they can make such changes for themselves.

What if you ask for guidance sincerely and without conditions, you listen carefully, but you still don't hear anything? Maybe you are being told to sit still, relax, rest, pull back, and be quiet. When you try too hard to make things work, you'll be told to sit back and smell the flowers so you can recharge and quiet the internal chatter that gets in the way of your being helped. Sometimes guidance says sit still and wait.

If you don't listen and watch carefully for divine guidance, you'll miss all the amazing doors put in front of you and all the wonderful possibilities open to you because you are looking for them in all the wrong places...like the rock music section.

CHAPTER 4

All About Angels
and Spiritual Guides

A spiritual guide is like a St. Bernard whose job is to rescue you from yourself, remind you of your connection to God, and help you evolve spiritually. I like to call these guides angels; others call them teachers, masters, or avatars. Whatever they are called, their purpose is the same: to help us when we ask for help. Angels are emissaries from God, ethereal beings who have had their metaphysical questions answered, seen life's mysteries unveiled, and possess complete and assured knowledge that God not only exists, but is on the job 24/7.

*   *   *

What do angels want us to know about them? First of all, angels serve at the pleasure of God. They are always available, eager to help, loving, gentle, kind, and powerful. Second, they have knowledge, an understanding, and a knowing of God that we can only pray for. They see through divine eyes, not human eyes, and have a much broader vision than we do.

While we tend to focus on ourselves and the small ripple effect we create a short distance around us, angels see the broader picture. Where we see a wave breaking on the Pacific shore, angels see the wave start in Japan and watch it cross the ocean until it reaches the shore. Because they see the bigger picture and we don't, their guidance doesn't always immediately make sense to us. But it is always for our highest good.

Angels have the ability to see the big picture – and to remind us about it. For example, imagine a driver cuts you off. You may react with anger or righteousness: "How dare he cut me off!" or "What a lousy driver!" The incident becomes focused on you and your judgment of the situation. Angels know that the man was rushing to his wife's side in the hospital; that he cut you off because he was distracted by his fear and grief over her condition.

Angels come in answer to your pleas for help. They are messengers from God that bring hope and remind you of your true spiritual nature, which is not separate from God. They change you for the better and teach you about gratitude.

Angels bring daily miracles into your life. They protect you, heal you, and guide you. They know you inside and out: your weaknesses and strengths, your fears and losses. They provide whatever your soul needs in order to learn and grow and evolve. And they can be summoned with one word: "Help!"

Wisdom

Please help me acquire wisdom by being open and willing to explore different ideas and beliefs. Let me hear Truth when it resonates with my soul and make choices that are good for me, even when my pride makes me stubbornly insist my way is better.

If you open your heart to God's unconditional love for you and learn to ask for help, you will allow angels into your life. They will transform you into a better person, full of integrity, forgiveness, and love. They will help you make better choices, guiding you toward God and away from your ego, pride, and old wounds.

When we know we have angels watching over

us, we don't respond with fear and self-righteousness. We can shift the focus from ourselves ("Look what happened to me") and pay attention to other people ("He's in a terrible hurry for some reason, let me pray for his safety").

Angels play many roles in our lives. They help, protect, guide, comfort, warn, teach, and give us the courage and inspiration to be better people. While they can come to us in many different ways—I have seen, heard, and felt angels—they always leave us feeling better than before they came. This was especially true for me one June day in New York.

*   *   *

One morning shortly after I'd finished college, I awoke to find the novel I had spent three years writing wiped clean from my computer. Even my backup disk was blank. I prayed to recover my precious book from whatever limbo it had gone into, but nothing happened. It had vanished without logical explanation.

I lay on the couch in my basement apartment in black despair, thinking about all the hard work that had been wasted. A part of my soul had gone into that book, and losing it felt like a traumatic amputation. I was heartbroken and wondered if I would ever write again. The only prayer I could utter was a plea for help with my despair.

Suddenly, a stranger in a blue-and-white striped polo shirt appeared at my screen door. I didn't know him, but he seemed so familiar I never thought to be afraid. His kind eyes drew me in, and I suddenly felt bathed in a pool of comfort. His smile was so warm and infectious, I found myself smiling back at him as I sat up. It still had not struck me that a strange man was standing there, but I was aware of how different I felt – how wondrously hopeful. I floated in the comfort he brought as he spoke just a few words.

"It will be okay, you will write again."

I stared at him, not certain if he had actually spoken or I had heard the words in my mind. When he turned to leave, I felt like all hope and love were being wrenched away. I jumped up from the couch and ran to the door. He was climbing the stairs to the driveway.

"Wait! What's your name?"

He turned and smiled. "Tom," he replied softly, and then continued on his way.

Hearing his name stopped me in my tracks momentarily as confusion, comfort, and excitement coursed through me. Then I threw open the door and raced up the short flight of steps…only to find him completely gone.

Behind him, though, Tom had left a definite imprint on me – one of joy, hope, and strength. I puzzled over this man. Who was he? How did he know I was sad? Why was he so darn familiar? It felt like I had received a gift, and I savored it even though I could make little sense of the encounter.

Shortly thereafter, I began to write again but in a very different way. My writing came more from my gut and my heart rather than my intellect. Expressing myself this way felt right and comfortable and true, and it still does to this day.

Years later, I mentioned this experience to one of my aunts. We were talking about God, and I said I was sure an angel had been sent to intervene in my life just when I needed one. When I described my apartment and my visit from "Tom the angel," as I always thought of him, my aunt became very quiet. Then she began to weep.

"What's wrong?" I ventured. "This was a great experience – it changed my life. Why are you crying?"

"I miss my father," she said quietly.

Then she took a deep breath and told me a story. It turned out that my aunt had lived in the

---

◇

Love

Please help me remember that I am always loved unconditionally and I can feel that love any time I choose to ask for it.

same exact apartment at the same exact age I had. During this time, she was in a period of deep sadness from missing her father, my grandfather, who had died. She felt quite alone and without direction in life. One night, while lying awake in bed crying and staring at the ceiling, she prayed for help. She felt a soothing presence on her shoulders, and was instantly comforted and filled with hope. She dried her tears and fell into a peaceful slumber.

I thought it was an interesting story. We had both lived in the same place at the same age. We had both asked for help and were brought great comfort at a time of great need. And we had both had such a profound feeling of peace, strength, and hope that we knew something miraculous had occurred.

But that wasn't the end of the story.

"Christel, you were very young when your grandfather died," my aunt said, taking my hand. "So you might not remember this, but his name was Tom – and he always wore a blue-and-white striped polo shirt."

*   *   *

I said at the beginning of this chapter that the job of an angel or spiritual guide is to rescue you from yourself, remind you of your connection to God, and help you evolve spiritually. Let me explain.

Your spiritual evolution depends on healing

your separation from God. You become separate when you believe you don't deserve God's unconditional love, you aren't worthy of receiving divine help, or you don't need it. If your pride insists that struggling through life on your own makes you a better person, you won't ask for God's help until you are at the end of your rope. Maybe not even then. If you need to be in control (or need to think you are in control) rather than live by divine guidance, you will lose sight of your connection to God and all the help available simply for the asking.

When you are aware of your connection with God, you feel like you have a flame of inspiration burning deeply and steadfastly within. That inspiration can feel like joy, contentment, artistic creativity, or a sense of peace deep within you. When you have drifted away from that flame, God feels far away even though at times you may experience a temporary easing of your despair or depression, or a small spark of joy amid your sadness.

Angels rescue you from yourself – from the separation from God caused by your own erroneous beliefs or pride – by taking whatever connection you do have with God and fanning that spark until it becomes a blazing fire. They do this by answering your prayers for help. The more you ask for help, the more you will receive it, and the more you will become aware of the presence of God in your life.

Asking for guidance brings you in touch with your soul – which is who you really are – a loving, kind being. Your soul or spirit is the part of you most like God. It is not concerned with your reputation or achievements or material wealth, but with your connection with the divine, which enhances your spiritual evolution.

Because they are spiritual beings, angels respond to the voice of your soul, not the needs of your ego. This is why an answer for help often seems to fly in the face of logic. Angels are not concerned with your pride or reputation or need for power — only with your highest good.

For example, a woman I know prayed for guidance because her ex-husband was spreading malicious lies about her several years after their divorce. In her prayer she asked, "What should I do about him?" The answer she got was, "Stay focused on God." This seemed like a strange answer to her because it didn't seem to address the problem.

But the angels knew better. The woman's real problem was not her ex-husband's lies. It was her attachment to her reputation. His lies were distressing her because she was concerned that other people would believe them. She thought that her worth depended on her reputation, and his lies would therefore diminish her worth.

This was exactly the problem the angels addressed when they replied, "Stay focused on God." When the woman focused on God, she felt God's love for her and knew her real worth. She was able to reconnect with her soul and embrace her true nature. This has allowed her to be of service to others and have an extremely positive ripple effect on those around her.

Said differently, she was able to spread love rather than resentment. Had she focused on anything but God when she felt damaged by her ex-husband's lies, her sense of low self-worth would not have been addressed and her ripple effect on others would have been one of shame, worry, and anger.

*   *   *

Grace

Please help me let go of what I think I need and be open to what God is trying to give me.

I know that some people believe there are important angels and lesser angels, but my experiences say there are not. When you die, angels comfort you and escort you to a "room" filled with other angels. There you are enveloped in light and suffused with joy. When I travel with the dying and stand at the threshold to this room, I can see that light inside and every angel is exactly the same. No one angel is brighter or bigger or more powerful than another. There is no receiving line with a pecking order of angels, just the brightest and most beautiful light. It beckons you to enter, add your own light to the celestial community, and immerse yourself in God's love.

Having seen that there are no greater or lesser angels, when I pray for help I don't measure the size of the job and request an accordingly-sized angel. I ask for help and receive it. If you get lost in trying to understand an angelic hierarchy, getting help will become a complicated process for you, delaying any intervention. Angels are all around us just waiting to help. They repeatedly tell me, "Ask and you will receive help." So just ask.

While angels do not have assigned jobs, our interactions with them feel different because our needs are different – and our needs do have a hierarchy. For example, when you are granted a small blessing, like finding a parking space in a crowded town, or being helped to arrive at an important interview on time, it's like a wave lapping against the shore of a secluded lake. You feel happy and grateful. On the other hand, when you are comforted by an angel so that your despair lifts or your sadness is replaced by joy, it's like being scrubbed clean and polished after being covered in mud. You feel like you are glistening with glory.

When you hear, feel, or see an angel, your spirit rejoices. Seeing an angel imprints you for life. It is an experience you will never forget, the memory of which will always bring you comfort, tears, laughter, or some other strong emotional response. This is because being visited by an angel goes deeper than anything else we have experienced in the context of our humanness. We are encountering the spirit of unconditional love and the energy of true forgiveness.

But please resist the urge to downplay the angel who parks your car because I have news for you. The angel that magnificently transports someone to the afterlife this evening was parking somebody's car this morning.

CHAPTER 5

Calling 911: I Need an Angel!

Many people have a concept of God as big and mysterious and vengeful. They hesitate to ask for guidance, even though I assure them God will welcome their request. These people find it much easier to ask for help from an intermediary, like an angel. So I am going to continue talking about guidance and angels. If that doesn't work for you, please substitute whatever term does, such as spiritual guides, helpers or masters, God, Higher Power, Goddess, or inner wisdom.

*   *   *

Communicating with angels is surprisingly easy. There are no special rules. It does not have to be a Sunday and you do not have to be wearing blue. You do not have to get on your knees. You simply call from your heart. Be sincere and you will get a response.

To call in an angel, simply ask for an angel to come to you, ask God to send you an angel, or ask for help from an angel. Then sit quietly and get clear about what you are going to ask your angel to do. Do you really want an answer to your question? Do you really want to feel comfort or reassurance or strength? Do you really want things to change? Once you know what you sincerely want and need, just ask for it.

Sometimes I've known exactly what I need, such as guidance or courage – or a parking space on a busy street. Yes, that's right. I have called upon my angels to help me park. Some people believe that angels have much more important things to do than help humans find parking spaces. That's like believing that St. Bernards should only rescue people in dire need. St. Bernards don't care. They don't judge whether you are a hapless soul, a fool, or a daredevil before deciding whether to come to your rescue. They just come. Every call for help matters to them. They have a job to do.

And so do those spiritual St. Bernards, your angels. The idea that an angel would judge you or your request for help is absurd. Your request is not forwarded to the Angel Committee and a vote taken on its worthiness. The function of angels is simply to help you. No job is too big or too small.

If you persist in thinking that angels should only intervene when your need is great, you are running a real risk. Even scientists now accept that our thoughts help create our reality. So do you want an abundance of miracles and angels in your life, or do you only want a few – and only when you need them really, really badly? Go for abundance! There's no such thing as an excess of angels.

When I'm not exactly sure what I need, but I know I could use help, I simply pray, "I need help!" After all, we're human. We don't always know what we need. Why waste time trying to figure it out? Especially when our angels are smarter, faster, and more far-seeing than we are. You can always let go and just ask for help. Trust that you'll be taken care of. Don't work so hard.

Once you've asked for an angel, then what? I said earlier that there were two prerequisites to working with angels: asking for help and being sincere in your request. That's true. But when the help arrives, you also have to open your eyes – and your mind – or you'll miss it. Unfortunately, we can become so focused on our own agenda that we neglect to notice help when it comes.

*   *   *

I confess to having done this during a spiritual

pilgrimage to Italy. At the Rome train station, my friend and I bought tickets to Assisi, home of St. Francis. Railway departures are notoriously precise in Italy. Trains waited for no man or woman, not even women on a spiritual journey.

After checking the track number and time of departure, we waited on Platform 18 for the train. I triple-checked the departures board for the train schedule and the assigned platform as the train pulled in. Everything was in order. But no sooner had we turned to board the train than hundreds of people – seemingly from nowhere – filled the platform. We couldn't reach the door of the car, though it was scarcely twenty feet ahead of us. The harder we tried, the more people filled our path. We were trapped.

I knew the train would not wait for us, yet getting to that door felt like a Herculean task. It was more than I could do. I prayed for God to help us board the train on time as I struggled with my rolling suitcase and blustered my way through the crowds until I found another place to climb on board. Those were the roughest steps I have ever taken. People banged into me, pushed me, and shoved me. Somewhere deep in my brain, this registered as strange. The Italian people are usually so friendly, so polite, yet for all the consideration they were giving us, we could have been invisible.

Finally, we climbed the four steps into the carriage, sweating but exhilarated to have triumphed in our struggle. Wrong. The aisle ahead was

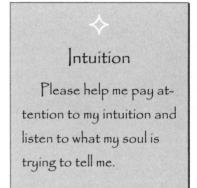

Intuition

Please help me pay attention to my intuition and listen to what my soul is trying to tell me.

bursting with people moving toward us. Again, something felt wrong. We had boarded through the door at the very head of the train. People should have been moving with us, toward the rear, not against us.

Our assigned seats were back in the third car. Determined I was, so I gathered my strength and courage and forged ahead, hollering to my friend, "Follow me!" We didn't get very far. My suitcase caught on everything and everyone. I said, "Excuse me, *scusi*, HELLOOO," but no one moved, and I could not make my way down the hallway. My friend called out, "Let's get off and try another car." We managed to climb off the train with absolutely no interference, but the platform was as crowded as it had been before. Checking the clock, I saw we had exactly four minutes before the train left. "Get back on," I shouted, "We'll find the right car after the train settles down."

Up those treacherous stairs we went, struggling with small suitcases that suddenly seemed much heavier and bigger and cumbersome. This would have been a great time to pay attention to what was happening, but I was focused on the goal: boarding the darn train.

Again the aisle was packed – where had all these people come from, and why weren't they in their seats? The train was leaving in two minutes. I took a breath and reminded myself that we had re-served seats and would eventually get to sit down somewhere. I asked God for help and let go of any attachment to the outcome of our trip. "It's in your hands, " I whispered. My friend spotted an opening in the sea of people and went for it. I followed her.

We panted our way six feet down the aisle when suddenly a large woman in the biggest fur coat I have ever seen came toward us with a look of Viking determination. I don't know what linebackers feel like the first time they are blocked, but that day I had a good idea. This woman meant business. She and her big fur coat bore down on us and literally pushed us backward toward the door through which we'd entered. All our "*scusi*'s" fell on deaf ears. She pushed us further and further until we were at the steps again. She didn't stop there. Her suitcase rolled over my friend's foot and jammed into my side. Her look said, "I'm not finished!"

"That's it," I hollered, "We're out of here. St. Francis is just going to have to wait. Get off the train before it starts moving." We hurried down the steps just as the train began to pull out of the station.

The platform was completely and utterly silent. The crowd had evaporated. On the train itself, no one was standing in the aisles of the car we just left. I got that weird shivery feeling and looked up to see the Viking woman in the fur coat smiling down at me as the train pulled out of the station. She didn't look so scary; in fact she was somehow comforting. I knew something important had happened, but I was so focused on my agenda of getting to Assisi that, as C.S. Lewis once put it, I was unaware of the profundity of the moment.

Sorely disappointed, we went to the ticket booth for a refund.

"But you will miss the train!" exclaimed the ticket clerk. "Do you not want to go to Assisi?"

"Of course we do. But…" I answered.

"Hurry to track eleven," he interrupted. "You have less than two minutes."

As it turned out, the railway authorities had

switched the track for the Assisi train and had neglected to update the departures board. The train we had been trying so hard to take was a non-stop express to Milan. Had we succeeded, we would have been trapped on a 300-mile train journey, stuck in Milan overnight, and missed our connections from Rome the next morning.

I thought of all our struggling and realized that had we gone with the flow – literally – we would never even have gotten aboard that train. I realized that angels had crowded that platform to prevent us from boarding, but because of our determination (or should I say stubbornness), we persisted. I even prayed for help! So the angel in the big fur coat had been sent. Trust me, she would have prevented the entire offensive line of the Dallas Cowboys from taking seats on that train. She had gotten us off the Milan express just in time. I had to laugh. How much more obvious could my guidance have been?

We can become so determined to achieve our goal that we neglect to see all the signs and help that surround us. Our focus becomes so narrow that we lose sight of the big picture. Angels are all around us. They never cease to offer guidance and help when we ask for it. We just have to look up and see them.

The next time you are doing something – preparing a meal, boarding a train, buying a lawnmower, or driving a car – and something feels like it's not working, seems too difficult, or is a struggle, look up from your task and ask to see the big picture. Angels are trying to tell you to slow down, ease up, get off, or let go.

Listen to them. Go with the flow. Stop sweating the unimportant or irrelevant stuff. Be grateful for the help and say thank you – for the parking space, the courage, or the escort into the afterlife.

CHAPTER 6

How Angels Communicate With Us

Have you ever run into someone who said exactly the thing you needed to hear? Sometimes it's an angel bringing comfort to your heart. Angels don't always take human form, but when they do, the scenario is always the same: the person who prayed sees, talks with, or is helped by someone who suddenly "disappears" and can't be found again. Physical descriptions of these angels are vague, but the wonderful feelings associated with their arrival are powerful and imprint us for life.

*   *   *

Some people feel angels or hear them, and some see them. Seeing an angel is something you will never forget. Just conjuring the image of the angel in the fur coat leaves me breathless with laughter. It's a clear reminder to not focus so much on my agenda but allow myself to be guided. Picturing Tom the angel always reminds me of the infinite love and comfort available to me during those nasty bumps in the road of life.

Angels are seen in other ways too. If you've ever had a near death experience, it's likely you've seen at least one angel. When I cross over with people, the space is so crowded with angels that their light is at once brilliant – almost blinding – yet soft, gentle, and comforting.

Having an angel whisper in your ear can be just as comforting. That happened one snowy night in January when I was taking a friend home.

I was driving a friend home when we hit a patch of black ice and I lost control of the car. "Help us! Protect us! Keep us safe!" I prayed. I spun the wheel in the proper direction to stop our skid, but it didn't work. We fishtailed back and forth across the busy two-lane highway. I should have been scared as we slid toward the tangle of cars directly in our path, but suddenly, I had an unusual feeling, like a breath of cold air upon my neck, that made me shiver. Then I heard a voice in my head say, "It will be okay."

In my mind's eye, I saw in slow motion the five-car accident that was about to happen. Even though I was powerless to change anything, I did not panic. I knew before the first car crashed that we would not be injured. In fact, I knew we would not be one of the five vehicles in the accident even though there were cars skidding on ice literally all around us. Somehow my Honda was protected and cradled as we passed straight through the chaos of cars slamming into each other and spinning out of control across both lanes of traffic. White-knuckled and wheezing, my friend turned to stare back at the devastation on the road behind us.

The next day she asked me, "Why didn't you panic when it looked like we were going to crash? Was it because of your E.R. training?"

"No," I replied. "It was because my angel told me not to worry. She said we'd make it through alright." To me it was so natural to hear an angel's voice in my head that I didn't stop to consider the impact of my explanation on my friend. She later acknowledged she had thought I was really weird at the time – but she did want to know more about angels.

*   *   *

Angels speak a distinct language: soft, heartfelt, vibrant, humorous, and powerful. They come when you pray for them, they come when you least expect them, and they come when you need them the most, especially in the E.R. I cannot count the number of times I saw angels visiting the people I nursed during my sixteen years as an E.R. and trauma nurse in New York.

Children often have an easier time seeing angels because they haven't been taught to ignore or fear them. Children accept angels and spiritual guides as a natural part of life. As indeed they are.

Even if you don't actually see an angel, there will be physical cues. Sometimes I feel a slight shiver inside of me; other times I hear a voice inside of my head or simply have a knowing about what to do or say. You can recognize an angel at work when you find yourself doing something kind or saying something wise that seems a bit out of character, and you wonder, "Where did that come from?"

Having an angel with you doesn't mean you'll escape accidents, injury, or death. But you will have a sense of calm, peace, and ease no matter how a situation plays out. You will face your challenges without being alone. And not being alone during a trial can make all the difference. This was profoundly evident the night baby Joseph was brought into my emergency room.

*   *   *

While working in the E.R., we often saw terrible tragedies – the deaths of children and parents, loss of limbs, gunshot and knife wounds, and the pain and suffering of those afflicted with illness. One evening in the E.R. was particularly difficult. Four-month-old baby Joseph was brought in without breath or heartbeat. I knew he would not survive and would be met on the other side by a slew of angels, so instead of praying for him, I prayed for an angel for his mother.

She was in shock and could barely stand as the huge stretcher carrying her tiny, utterly still baby was rolled into the E.R. Nurses and doctors lined every inch of the stretcher, from top to bottom. Their anxious faces intensified as the hospital operator announced a Pediatric Code Blue over the P.A. system.

The E.R. staff dropped everything and prepared for baby Joseph. Prayers were silently whispered, oaths were sworn, and each of us sucked in air and held it when we saw the child. Babies are supposed to be pink and cute, but baby Joseph was blue and bloated. With two huge fingers, a doctor was pressing on the baby's chest, squeezing the heart between sternum and backbone. A tube thinner than a straw was inserted into his little mouth and down his trachea to bring oxygen to his breathless lungs. It was all to no avail.

I took the dreaded walk to find his mother. She wasn't hard to spot among the twenty to thirty people in the waiting room. Her gaze was glued to me, anxious for my eyes to meet hers. Those last few steps across the room to her side were the worst. I wanted to take her to the privacy of the Quiet Room and talk to her there, preserving the dignity of her grief, but it was not to be.

At first baby Joseph's mother thought I was being nice and just giving her a break from the crowd in the waiting room. But I knew that when she went into that room, she would lose her son, and soon she knew it too. She hesitated in the doorway, pierced my soul with her eyes, and would go no further.

In giving her the bad news about her baby, I was supposed to follow a script and start by gently inferring that the boy's situation was grave, even though in reality there was no hope for him. I was supposed to break the news slowly, but I knew I was evading the truth, and my eyes betrayed me.

"Tell me," she whispered. "Tell me the truth."

I silently shook my head no, and she collapsed into my arms. Wrenching sobs tore through her body, as the doctor spotted us. He motioned for me to take the woman into the Quiet Room, but I raised my eyebrows, indicating defeat. Then the woman lifted her head from my shoulder. Mascara had run down both cheeks and she looked utterly helpless. I wrapped my arm protectively around her shoulders and squeezed as the doctor began his rehearsed lines:

He told her that baby Joseph's heart still wouldn't beat on its own, and explained how the brain begins to die when deprived of oxygen for longer than four minutes. Then he claimed he didn't know what the outcome would be.

The woman took a deep breath and asked if her son was dying. The doctor gave a pat reply about doing everything he could.

"I want to hold his hand," she said. "I don't want him to die alone."

I nodded my head and the doctor shot me a warning look. He advised her against it and started to leave. When I opened my mouth to protest, he silenced me with a glance.

I left the woman weeping into her hands and returned to the Code Room. No progress had been made as CPR continued on baby Joseph; that little heart just refused to beat. I moved close to the doctor and told him in a low voice that the mother had the right to be with her baby. He looked at me with disbelieving eyes and asked if I could really subject her to this sight.

Kindness

Please help me take that extra step and be kind to others. Help me to be aware of their needs and pray for them daily.

I looked at the blue and bloated form on the stretcher
– but all I saw was a dying child who needed his
mother.

I returned to baby Joseph's mother. I knew she
was determined to see her child, and I felt she had
the right to be with him. I prayed for an angel to be
with her, to comfort her and bring her strength. I
knew the baby would be met in the afterlife; in fact,
he was already surrounded by angels. It was her I
was worried about.

I brought the woman to her baby's side. I explained the tubes and the procedures that were going on. She sat quietly holding his tiny hand, oblivi-
ous to the crowd of doctors and nurses and aides,
the blood on the sheets, and those two huge fingers
pushing on that tiny chest. She looked to the doctor,
asking silently if there was any hope. He shrugged
his shoulders and gave the scripted reply, "We're
doing everything we can."

At that instant I felt a surge in the air and something changed – baby Joseph's mother shifted from
shock and despair to an almost ethereal calm. She
looked as though she were listening to someone
whispering in her ear. I found out later that she had
prayed for an angel at the very same moment I had.

She had been painfully torn between wanting us
to continue life-saving measures or telling us to stop

the CPR. She knew deep down there was no hope, but she couldn't bear to be the one who ended her child's life. So she had asked for an angel to help her be strong and take loving care of her baby.

Suddenly the room took on a shimmer of energy that signaled an answer to her prayer. She glanced at the doctor as if she were seeing him for the first time. Her face changed, and I could see strength in her that had not been there before. She said she didn't want her baby to suffer anymore, and asked the doctor to stop CPR.

Several faces expressed shock, but she didn't see them. She never took her eyes from baby Joseph. The doctor tried to convince her to rethink her decision, but she only shook her head and said she couldn't allow any more suffering.

The room seemed to divide in that instant between those who agreed with her and those who felt she was giving up too soon – this was a baby boy, after all, not a ninety-nine-year-old man. Everyone looked to the doctor to see what he would do, when suddenly the mother reached out and gently took the big hand doing CPR into her own, and said, "Please, no more." Time slowed as her words lingered. No one moved or spoke. Even if there had been a gun at each of our heads, none of us would have restarted the CPR.

I watched baby Joseph's spirit rise from his body in glorious freedom. For an instant he hovered in that room and then was gone. Oddly, it was almost beautiful. "It was the angel," she told me later, "that steadied my hand to stop CPR. I didn't think I had the strength to do it and suddenly I saw myself doing it."

No one spoke but I noticed a few raised eyebrows. The disbelievers had shown themselves. I asked everyone to leave the room before I bathed baby Joseph. For more than an hour his mother rocked him on her breast, quietly whispering sweet nothings. It was an angel that brought her peace with her decision, and an angel that gave her hope that she would make it through this terrible ordeal.

*   *   *

It's not only the sad circumstances where we find angels. Help is available to us on an "as needed" basis. However, many times, angels comfort and heal us in ways different from what we expect. We might pray for one thing and receive something totally different. This is the time to let go of control and trust the spiritual help so readily available. When we are open to the help in all its forms, we discover that God can make us smile in even the darkest of times.

After finally listening to my guidance to leave

my beloved job in the E.R. and use my intuitive gifts
full-time, I moved from New York to California. But
my leap of faith got me no parades – nor an answer
to, "What's next?" How was I supposed to get
started? How was I going to support myself? I
thought that having followed my guidance, I de-
served some specific answers from God or my angels. When no answers were forthcoming, I began to
second-guess my decision to quit my job.

One afternoon I went down to the beach to pon-
der the empty silence that had replaced my once-
resounding guidance. I felt alone, out on a limb,
without the angelic comfort I needed.

When I arrived at Moonlight Beach, I was an-
noyed to find hordes of people milling around. I was
feeling alone and I wanted to be alone. Looking
south, I spotted a quiet, empty stretch about 250
yards away, and made my way there. As I headed
toward this sanctuary, I silently dared anyone to
stop me. I was feeling more than a little surly about
all the people impinging on my solitude.

Fortunately, my inner turmoil was bigger than
my pride, so as I walked, I prayed for God to send an
angel to comfort me. I needed to be reminded that I
was on the right path. I settled down on the sand, sat
back, relaxed, and watched the soothing rise and fall
of the waves – until a man walked up and squarely

blocked my view. Anger spurted through me. I was about to shoo him away when he spoke.

"What do you think you're doing?" he demanded. "You can't be here."

His attitude was defiant and I was in no mood for dealing with

> ✦
>
> # Laughter
>
> Please help me to remember to laugh at myself and not take my life so seriously. Help me to see the humor in all situations.

a pain in the ass. "It's the only place around here without people," I answered.

He looked at me strangely. "How did you get here?" Then he added, "You can't stay."

I was in no mood for silly questions or to be told I couldn't sit on a free beach. I was about to issue a less-than-friendly retort, when I suddenly noticed there were eight or ten people standing on the sand nearby. Guards surrounded them and a barricade held back the hordes of people I'd seen earlier. Then a woman walked past and gave me a smile.

I was filled with joy as I recognized her and waved back. Then I took in the whole of my situation and began to laugh.

My prayer had been answered. I had somehow

gotten past the security guards and parked myself smack in the middle of the filming of an episode of "Touched by an Angel." And the comforting smile I received had come, of course, from "Monica," one of the show's two angels.

CHAPTER 7

Grace – and Angels – to the Rescue

By the grace of God, help is available to you anytime you ask, whether you are in an emergency or simply in a quandary. Grace is being loved by God without doing anything to earn it. Grace is also being unable to do anything to lose that love. You can turn your back on grace and refuse to accept it, but you can't ever lose it. The most you can do is temporarily separate yourself from God's love by denying it exists, insisting you don't deserve it, believing you must do something to earn it, or refusing to ask for help when you need it.

*   *   *

You may find that believing in angels or asking for guidance, gets you "kicked out" of what I call your tribe – by which I mean your family, teachers, and religious institutions. Angels will still take care of you. Angels love you unconditionally even when others do not. In fact, angels love you even when you are not sure you love yourself. I learned this valuable lesson one evening in July many years ago.

While slowly coming into acceptance of my intuitive gifts, I struggled with my relationship with the Catholic Church, in which I had been raised. According to the church, seeing the future or having gifts such as clairvoyantly seeing where illness is in the body, reading someone's energy field or aura, and viewing a running "video" of their past is an abomination.

Activities like these are considered profoundly evil. I knew that accepting the truth of my gifts and deciding to use them – even for good – would make me an outcast in my church. When we break the rules of our tribe and decide to leave it, we are never given a cake brightly inscribed with "Congratulations on leaving the tribe!" Rather, it's a time of rejection – or worse.

In a moment of indecision I went to

✧

Self-Acceptance

Please help me be at peace with who I am and revel in my true self – a child of God who is loved unconditionally.

---

speak to a priest about my dilemma: was I evil or was I blessed? Our conversation was quite brief. When I began to outline my problem, he quickly stood and raised his arm, index finger pointing at me as though warding off evil. "Get out!" he roared. "You are demon spawn. Never return to the church."

These are pretty intense words to hear when you have just turned twenty-one, but they did not devastate me (though, needless to say, I did not step foot in a Catholic church for a long, long time). I know my angels stood with me that day, hands upon my shoulders, protecting me from the full brunt of the priest's betrayal. The pain of that rejection could have devastated me, creating doubts and fears and causing me to abandon my gifts. It did not. My angels made it clear that my intuition was a gift from God, and therefore it couldn't be evil. They made it clear that I was loved regardless of what this man said and regardless of how my tribe reacted to my God-given gift. I became grateful instead of fearful, and my wound began to heal quickly.

Eventually I realized it was the priest's fear and ignorance that spoke to me, not God's voice, and that he was a human and therefore fallible. I felt compassion for his fearful state and saddened by his rigidity. And I was able to laugh at his pastoral listening and counseling skills – they sucked.

My angels restored my respect for myself, cushioned my "fall" from the church, and helped me see past one man so that when I was ready I could regain the rituals of comfort and the tradition of community that the church offers. This experience showed me that it's not always physical perils that the angels protect us from. Sometimes it's psychological or emotional harm.

Not that my angels haven't been called upon to prevent me from physical harm over the course of the years. I have an adventurous streak and I love to travel, two traits that have given them plenty of opportunity to save my life.

*　　　*　　　*

When I finished my second bachelor's degree, I gave myself the gift of a trip to the Grand Canyon. I met up with a group who planned to descend the canyon in late morning and I excitedly joined them. Hiking down the Bright Angel Trail was spectacular and taxing in the early June sun. The weather is extremely unpredictable at the canyon: one minute it is a blazing 100 degrees while the next, hail the size of golf balls is falling from the sky. Twenty minutes into the hike I felt rumblings in my stomach that quickly turned into pain. I knew I couldn't continue and, severely disappointed, I returned to my cabin and rested for the remainder of the day. That evening there was a buzz of activity on the rim. I learned that one of the other hikers had fallen from the trail and been badly injured. She was airlifted to a trauma center. Hearing this, I felt a tingle inside and realized it could have been me. I prayed for her – and prayed gratitude for my own safety.

The second day, a friend and I hopped on the canyon mules for a ride down to the Colorado River. The mules are bred for this type of journey (and I swear they have a sense of humor to boot). On the way down, the right side of the trail is cliff, rock, and canyon formation, while the left side is a drop straight down – very, very far down.

The mules love to walk on the outside edge and when they walk, of course, only two of their hooves are on the ground at any given time. And one of those two hooves is on sand that was crumbling beneath their immense weight. It feels like they're going to slide over the edge or the edge will crumble from their weight, sending mule and rider plummeting to the canyon floor.

By the time we safely reached the Colorado River, I was tense to say the least. It was hot but beautiful. I looked up to the top of the Canyon and thought, "The trip up must surely be easier and safer than the trip down." Was I ever wrong.

After lunch we began our ascent under gorgeous blue skies. The trail leader came first, then me on "Miss Jane," followed by my friend and fifteen others. The expansiveness of the canyon was mesmerizing – my spirit felt like it was soaring without restraint. I was drinking in the other-worldliness of the Canyon when I got a premonition of danger. I snapped back to the reality that while beautiful, the canyon could also be deadly. I scanned ahead to the switchbacks leading to the rim. There were hikers ascending, people taking pictures, and our group riding mules. Everything looked fine. I relaxed in my saddle but the prickly feeling persisted.

Suddenly, I heard our leader's radio blaring a flash flood warning. Just as I was pondering how cloudless skies could cause flash floods, rain exploded overhead. Worried, our guide hollered back at us, "Get a move on, and keep your mules nose-to-tail!" He had to get us out of the canyon before the heavy rain caused mudslides.

We pulled our rain parkas over our heads and huddled tightly onto the mules. They plodded along fairly quickly but had to be rested every so often. Our guide's nervous face only heightened our anxiety.

The wind picked up and began to howl past our hoods, while the rain blinded us to all but the four feet of trail immediately ahead. I prayed for a host of angels to protect us, but…I heard it just before I saw it: a deep rumbling followed by a flash as blue as the sky. I heard the word "Stop!" in my mind and halted my mule, which stopped everyone behind me. The leader turned around and screamed, "Get Miss Jane moving, NOW!" But I was rooted to the spot. I couldn't move. As he began to turn his mule around to come back and grab my reins, I screamed "Watch out!"

In that instant, a huge boulder came crashing in front of us, barely a foot ahead of him. The mules shied, and the situation almost unraveled as the realization that our guide had nearly been swept away by a crashing boulder dawned on each of us.

Shaken but determined to get to the top, we pushed our mules upward as the flash flooding began. We had just reached the ridge when the sky opened with thunder, lightening, and huge hail stones. Fifteen minutes later, the storm was gone and the blue, blue sky had returned.

The leader asked me what had made me stop and call out to him. I told him. He looked deeply into my eyes and said, "Thank you…you saved my life." He had not heard the rumbling and never saw the boulder coming. I later learned that the flash of blue I had seen was a young woman in a blue parka who had been swept over the cliff by that same boulder. She had died almost instantly.

Twice I had been protected on the trail, and twice people were hurt. I had a choice: I could wonder, "Why them and not me?" Or I could spend my time in gratitude, and follow the guidance given me by my angels and share this story with you.

Often I am asked, "Why do angels intervene sometimes and not others?" That question comes from a human narrow perspective. When a child is sick and dies, for example, it doesn't mean his angel didn't show up. I know for a fact that angels met that child at the doorway to the next realm. Have you ever noticed how very sick children often have a sense of peace about them? They are still more apt to laugh, than adults. They don't question their mental state when an angel comes: they simply

---

✧

Help

Please give me strength and courage and lead me to a place of serenity. Help me to soften my heart and feel your loving presence.

enjoy it and savor the company.

It's our choice whether to make something positive out of cruel circumstances. I often think of the good done by John Walsh, creator and host of "America's Most Wanted" and primary mover behind the founding of the National Center for Missing & Exploited Children. His work on behalf of missing children began after his own six-year-old son, Adam, was kidnapped from a shopping mall and found murdered sixteen days later. Adam's killer has never been found.

I don't believe that God or the angels pick and choose who will die and who will be saved. We live in a world in motion where human misery and tragedy is largely the result of man's actions and choices. But we do have access to help from beyond our human perspective. This doesn't mean everyone will survive terrible car crashes or diseases. It doesn't mean that bad things won't happen to us or our children. But it does mean there is help available to us, if we are open to believing in that help and we ask for it.

CHAPTER 8

When Angels Visit You
in Your Dreams

If you are sincere in what you are asking for and have put no conditions on your request, but you still hear nothing, ask for guidance to come in your dreams. For some people, this is the easiest way to access guidance and help from their angels. Maybe it's because when we are asleep, our angels don't have to work so hard to get through to us.

*　　　　*　　　　*

As you know, I was working as an E.R. nurse when I was clearly given guidance to quit my job and use my intuitive gifts full-time. The problem was, I didn't want to. For a while I negotiated with God by keeping my job but doing intuitive readings on the side. I received great satisfaction from my E.R.

work, had climbed the ladder of success, and didn't want to jump down from it.

From the outside, it probably looked as if things were going great in my life. But they weren't. Although I loved nursing, I didn't derive life-enhancing energy from my job anymore. There was a nursing shortage at the time, and I went home each night feeling drained from having to make so many difficult life-or-death choices on every shift.

The pivotal event for me was a night shift when a five-year-old with epiglottis in extremis (the airway is blocked due to swelling) was brought in. Literally one minute later, a 55-year-old man with a lethal cardiac arrhythmia arrived. Both conditions are life-threatening, both require immediate one-on-one care, and both patients would die without intervention. Unfortunately, there was only one E.R. physician and one RN – me. The rest of the staff there that night were unlicensed aides. Life-threatening conditions initially require at least two licensed professionals to stabilize a patient—aides are not qualified to give medications, triage, or perform life-saving interventions other than CPR.

So I did the only thing I could. I told an aide to push the cardiac-arrest alarm in both patients rooms, knowing that it would awaken all the residents sleeping upstairs. It worked, and both patients pulled through. What I didn't do was get the message that my angels were trying to send me that night: "You can't do this job anymore; the situation is untenable and it is draining your vital energy."

Since I didn't get it, my angels had to amp up the signal.

After that stressful night, I began to have a recurring dream, which I named the Blood Lake dream. In the dream I was on a bus with many people. Suddenly the bus stopped at a lake and we all got off. There were two paths around the lake. Many people took the path to the right. As I started to follow them, a man with kind eyes pointed to the left and told me to go the other way.

Mesmerized by the aura of love surrounding this man, I turned and went with him toward the left-hand path. Suddenly I heard a moan coming from the right. As a nurse, I felt compelled to find out what was wrong and offer my assistance. When I stepped away from the kind man, he gently took hold of my arm and shook his head, "No." He gestured for me to continue down the left-hand path. I felt torn. Then I heard the moan again, much louder this time.

I apologized to the kind man and started walking to the right. The sadness I saw in the man's eyes was so deep, the memory of it haunts me to this day. As I walked away, I couldn't shake the feeling of his eyes on my back, but I strode determinedly toward the right-hand path around the lake. The moans and wails of suffering became louder and more pitiful. The farther I walked, the less color I saw. Everything became a dull gray.

I reached the person who was moaning. He was severely injured and in great pain. His wounds were bleeding profusely and draining into the lake. It was then that I realized the lake was filled with blood. As I tended to the wounded man, I heard more moans and cries for help. The pain and agony of the other injured people echoed across the lake. Each time I would stop to help someone, another victim would cry out in need. There was no one to help me so I began triaging the best I could, aiding those who seemed most likely to survive and leaving the most desperately wounded to their fate.

The number of victims increased, their pain was extreme, and I knew I could no longer decide to help one and not another. In anguish, I cried out, "I can't play God!" I couldn't decide who should be helped and who shouldn't, who would have his pain relieved and who wouldn't.

Suddenly I saw an escalator on the path. I jumped on and rode it upward. The higher I went, the more color returned to my surroundings. When I stepped off the escalator I found myself in the middle of Macy's department store, surrounded by colorful and festive Christmas decorations. There were carolers, exquisite gifts, and tinseled trees all around me. It was the biggest Christmas display I had ever seen. In that moment of joy and relief, I awoke from my dream.

I know now that the kind man in my dream was an angel trying to steer me in the direction that was in my highest good. I know this because I recognized the love for me in his eyes and the sadness he felt when I ignored him. The Christmas display inside of Macy's was a metaphor for the peace and joy I would have in my life if I left Blood Lake (the E.R.) and followed my angel's guidance.

At the time, though, this dream both mystified me and shook me to my core. How could I choose who got help and who didn't without violating my soul? I prayed to understand the dream's meaning. The message was obvious, of course, but because I didn't want to hear it, I didn't hear it. Instead I analyzed the escalator ride and Christmas at Macy's, looking for symbols.

The dream continued for months, and the months turned into years. And I continued to ignore the obvious. Finally the dream became so frequent and so stressing that one night I prayed to be

relieved of it. My prayer was answered, but not quite
in the way I had hoped for. That night I had a dream
that left me more traumatized than a car crash. I
dreamed I fell one hundred stories down an elevator
shaft and died. When I awoke, I was lying on the
floor of my room, unable to move or open my eyes.
It felt as though every bone in my body was broken.
In this "road kill" state I heard a booming voice
ordering, "Quit the ER and use your gifts full-time!!"

I didn't. The Blood Lake dream returned with a
vengeance. The more I tried to negotiate with God so
I could stay in the E.R., the more I had the dream.
Sometimes I would awake in a cold sweat, feeling
completely wrung out from all the triaging I had
been forced to do at the lake's edge. Exhausted, I
would pray for help. But I always heard the same
response. God never wavered. Over and over, the
voice said, "Leave your job." Eventually I listened.

My angels had worked tirelessly to get me to see
the light. When I didn't heed their message in my
waking life, they came to me in my dreams. Once I
finally listened to my guidance and embraced my
intuitive gifts full-time, I began walking a path (the
left-hand one, no doubt) that has brought me
tremendous peace and joy. My life still has
occasional bumps in the road, but mostly, every day
feels like Christmas.

Our dreams, while not always pleasant are a form of communication from the spirit world. They can be a warning of imminent danger, a portent of what is to come, an answer to a prayer, or simply another way of sending us guidance. Fortunately, I am not always that obtuse about the messages from my angels that arrive in dreams – even if the dreams are someone else's.

On my last day of vacation in the Bahamas, I decided to go parasailing. For some reason, I called home to check in. I found my mom rather distracted, only half listening to my adventures.

"What's wrong?" I asked.

She took a deep breath and began, "I had a strange dream and I don't understand it. There was a multicolored…I don't know…it looked like parachute floating in the air. Then I saw a rope dangling."

The hair on my arms stood up.

"It really shook me up," she said. "Please don't go near anything like that, okay?"

I hung up. A chill

> ✦
>
> Personal Power
>
> Please help me step forward with integrity in all areas of my life and acknowledge my innate strengths and abilities.

climbed up my spine. It sounded like she'd seen the bright colors of a parasail that had lost its rider.

Then my skeptical, rational mind kicked in, and I went to the beach anyway. I watched a man who was strapped into the harness of a parasail rise effortlessly into the sky, and I reveled at the thought of flying like that. I wanted to know what it felt like. But something inside held me back. My mother's dream had gotten to me.

In the next instant, I saw that the wind had kicked up, and the men driving the parasail tow boat were trying to pull their rider quickly back to shore. Suddenly the guide rope broke, and the man in the harness dangled like a rag doll in the hand of a running child. I watched in horror as the wind swept him into the side wall of the hotel. His chute crumpled and he fell several hundred feet to his death.

*   *   *

My mother's psychic ability was well known in our neighborhood. She used to astound her friends with her accuracy. This gift was passed down to me, and when I had a prophetic dream warning of danger to my mother, she didn't hesitate to listen.

I awoke one day in a cold sweat from the second-most-vivid dream in my life: I watched in horror as my mom crossed a street and was hit by a

white car. I saw her fly across the hood and smash
into the ground. I heard the roar of the speeding car
and the terrible sound of her bones breaking. I felt
like I was inside her as her blood seeped onto the
pavement. I felt pain, then no pain. She was dead.

I grabbed the phone and called her at the condo
where she was vacationing in Hawaii, even though it
was only 5:00 a.m. there.

"Well, hi," she said brightly. "You just caught
me. I was on my way out the door."

"Don't go outside," I screamed. Words tumbled
breathlessly from my mouth. I described the street I
had seen in my dream, the surrounding buildings,
and the sidewalk. Even though I had never been to
Hawaii and knew nothing about the condo my
mother had rented, my description was completely
accurate.

"But why don't you want me to go outside?" my
mother asked.

"Because I saw you crossing that street and
being hit by a car."

Silence filled the line. Finally my mother said in
a small voice, "Every morning I go across the street
to buy the morning paper. I was just opening the
door to go when you called."

CHAPTER 9

Spiritual Evolution Takes Only One Lifetime

Angels have a wonderful effect on us – not just because they help us when we ask for help, but because their positive energy raises our own energy. As they say, we are known by the company we keep. Angels can actually speed your spiritual growth.

*　　　*　　　*

When I say "positive energy," I am talking about the actual electromagnetic energy that we, like all living things, emit. This energy, which is present in every cell in our body, radiates from us in the form of vibrations. When the frequency of your vibration is high, you have "positive energy."

So, although we are all beings of flesh and

blood, we are much more than that. We are beings of energy, and we all run at a particular vibration – some people much higher or lower than others. High vibration is synonymous with health, happiness, love, joy, and passion. A low vibration is synonymous with illness, hatred, resentment, revenge, and jealousy. We all make choices daily – consciously and unconsciously – that either raise or lower our vibration. People who choose to forgive and feel compassion have a high vibration. People who choose to be narrow-minded and spiteful have a much lower vibration. Also, associating with low-vibration people or being in an abusive relationship can and will lower your vibration.

As I said at the opening of this chapter, asking your angels for help can significantly raise your vibration. Being around their high vibration moves us. Our souls recognize this goodness and want to emulate it because it is our natural state – we must work diligently to be otherwise. The uplifting of our spirits is an actual rise of our overall vibration.

Have you ever noticed how you respond to happy people who are smiling? You feel good around them and tend to be uplifted into their happiness. What about when you are around a playful person, don't you feel more playful, light, and fun? Now compare that with being around a forgiving person – you've seen them on talk shows or perhaps are lucky enough to know one personally – where a mother forgives a someone for driving drunk and killing her child. Are you not in awe and is not your compassion and desire to forgive awakened to some degree?

Positive energy is contagious. When you are around a profound role model, you can't help but want to strive to be a better person and emulate the qualities of that person. Can you imagine standing before the Dalai Lama or Mother Teresa and feeling resentful or self-important? The high vibration of others compels us to rise above petty jealousies and feuds, to replace resentment with forgiveness. We become swept away in the high vibration, which is infinitely more pleasant than a low one.

This is why angels change you on such a deep level. God is the highest vibration of all. It's the vibration of unconditional love. How can you interact with a spiritual liaison to God and be anything but changed for the better?

No matter how bad our situation, we are never without the option to raise our vibration. Asking for guidance or calling for help from our angels is a choice available to everyone at every moment. In addition, the guidance we receive will often come at a much higher vibration than the one the prayer is on. This means it will be for your highest good, no matter what you prayed for.

Living at a high vibration is the secret to spiritual growth. If you want to raise your vibration, start by making simple requests for help from your spiritual guides, seeking out high-vibration people, and doing things that raise your vibration, such as praying, lighting candles, singing, dancing, laughing, or playing with a pet.

If you choose to be compassionate or forgiving by letting go of your past hurts and living in the present, your vibration will continue to rise. Should you associate with loving, tender, good-humored, and gentle souls, and choose not to gossip or bad-mouth others, your vibration will begin to soar. The last step in spiritual growth is to choose to look at your shadow, the buried and unconscious part of yourself that drives your behavior, lowers your vibration, and prevents you from achieving your dreams. When you explore your shadow, you may not like everything you see, but you always have the choice to change it. That's what spiritual responsibility – which we'll talk more about in a moment – is all about: making the choice to change whatever is not working in your life, including parts of yourself!

Our choices are what ultimately determine our

vibration and the rate of our spiritual growth. And sometimes those choices can save our lives.

*   *   *

As a youngster I had a great fear of death, which increased dramatically after I went to see "Night of the Living Dead."

> ✦
>
> ## Pleasure
>
> Please help me learn to enjoy myself and do what's best for my spirit. Teach me my limitations and guide my heart and mind in making decisions.

You'd never find me in a graveyard at night. Show me a coffin and my hair stood up on my arms. Even though I swore off horror films early on, my fear of the unknown lingered and deepened, thanks to my rampant imagination.

None of this was on my mind, however, when I was traveling in Egypt with a friend, and we decided one night to see the sarcophagus at the top of the Great Pyramid of Giza, one of the original seven wonders of the world. We had been forewarned that at midnight, the lights inside the pyramid would go out for thirty minutes, and we planned to be back outside before that. Having made it to the top and seen the amazing King's Burial Chamber with its huge red granite sarcophagus, we started back down the passageway. The corridor was fairly rugged and lacked the safety rails or helpful signs found in American tourist attractions. But at least it was decently lit.

Wrong. The tomb keeper's watch must have been fast because suddenly we were plunged into total blackness and silence. Only a little daunted, we continued our precarious descent guided by feel alone. Inching our way along the many twists and turns, we held hands, duck-waddling under the low earthen roof. I literally couldn't see my hand in front of my face. I asked God to send a few angels to guide us safely to the exit. I remembered from our trip up that there was a very dangerous section where the path turned sharply to avoid a drop of about thirty feet, but I had no idea how close to it we were.

Making our way in pitch black darkness was both tedious and nerve-wracking – until suddenly I realized where I was and began to laugh. The echoes of my laughter off the stone walls only made me laugh more. My friend thought I had lost my mind.

"Christel," she whispered, "are you okay?"

At this point tears were streaming down my face, and the more I tried to speak, the louder I howled.

"It's okay," she soothed, "We'll get out. You'll

be okay."

I only laughed harder and sputtered, "I'm okay!"

"You are?"

"Yes," I managed. I took a few breaths, and between smothered giggles and howls, I said "What's the thing I am most terrified of?"

Without hesitation she replied, "Coffins and graveyards."

"And where are we now?"

"In the largest Giza pyrami…" Then she burst into laughter, too, which set me off again.

"We are in the world's largest graveyard, in complete darkness, with an ancient and spooky coffin upstairs! It could only happen to you. How do you feel?"

"Fantastic, other than the fact that now I have to go to the bathroom badly, plus we are on a very dangerous section in the pitch dark," I replied, my sides aching from laughing so hard.

We continued our way down even more slowly as our giggling made the route twice as treacherous. Suddenly I had a very strong intuition to stop. In fact, I could not have moved if I wanted to. My legs felt like lead and my body sank down into the dirt. This otherworldly feeling was not foreign to me – I had experienced it a few times before. I grabbed my friend's hand.

"Let's wait here until the lights come back on."

So she sat down next to me, and we dangled our feet over the ledge we were on. Our hands were scraped and bruised, our clothes dusty and dirty. Then we heard a movement in the dark.

"Rats," I whispered. We froze. Suddenly nothing was funny anymore.

Then we noticed a small light moving toward us. A tomb guard had heard our screams of laughter and thought we were in trouble. So he used the only light available to look for us: a tiny Bic lighter. He found us clinging to each other, white-faced and stock still.

He was terribly proud to have rescued us and bragged to the other guards when we got back outside. He was a hero, so we didn't explain that our hysteria was laughter, not fear. When the lights came back on, I realized I had left my jacket on the ledge. When I went in to retrieve it, I was able to see where we had been sitting. We had taken a wrong turn – the flimsy cord that served as a guardrail was missing – and we were one step away from falling head-first into an empty shaft thirty feet deep.

I prayed gratitude that night for my friend, my guardian angel, my ability to laugh at myself, the absence of rats, and our safety – but most of all for

God's sense of humor, which was not lost on me.

*   *   *

When we regularly communicate with angels, we tend to effortlessly make better choices that make us happy, healthy, and more spiritually evolved. This is because we are operating at a higher vibration.

When your vibration increases, you sometimes find

Spiritual Responsibility

Please help me take responsibility for what I have chosen in life by letting go of my need to be a victim and making choices that improve my life, erase doubt and worry, and remind me that guidance is always there for me.

yourself saying something kind to a complete stranger for no apparent reason. Other times you feel very comfortable with who you are. You have more self-esteem and more courage. You laugh more. Pain lessens and despair lifts. There is a natural desire to be of service that overshadows fears or doubts.

Doing a reading on someone with a high vibration is always a delight for me. Aside from the pure pleasure of being around someone like that, the colors I see in their energy field are more exciting than a Fourth of July fireworks display. There is a 3-D quality with brighter colors and an almost explosive and tangible joy that infuses my heart and causes a tingling of fun and smiles inside of me.

Earlier I mentioned the steps you can take to raise your vibration and achieve spiritual growth. Eventually, you will yearn for more than growth. You'll aim for true spiritual evolution. What's the difference? I see spiritual growth as something we work on day by day, while spiritual evolution is what we do over the course of our lives by living in a perpetual state of high vibration. Here's an example: when we are working on our spiritual growth and a cashier hands us $5 too much in change, we look at it, think it over, and decide if we are going to say anything to her about it. When we have made a step in our spiritual evolution, we don't even hesitate – we simply hand it back without any debate, conflict, regret – or even self-congratulation.

The process of spiritual evolution is actually quite simple. The first part of the process is to accept spiritual responsibility for your life. This means that you take responsibility for the current state of your life, for your choices, and for their consequences, no matter what illness, wounds, or problems you have and no matter who or what caused them. You do this by living in the moment, being honest about what you want, and choosing not to be a powerless victim.

Accepting spiritual responsibility means realizing that there are no mysteries as to why your life is the way it is. You understand the connection between the choices you have made and the results in your life. You are not mystified or wonder why your positive thoughts aren't producing positive effects. You'll know that secretly you are harboring victim or blaming others energy, that says, "poor me, my life is this way because of other people."

Does this sound like a hard path to take? You might be surprised to hear that people have told me that when they took spiritual responsibility for their lives, they breathed easier. It was like having a weight removed from their shoulders. All of a sudden, they were no longer at the mercy of others or their past. They didn't need someone else to change in order to be happy. They were truly the captain of their own ship. No wonder they felt relieved.

The second part of the process of spiritual evolution is listening to your soul and making choices that bring you closer to God. Your ability to hear your soul's desires and make such choices is dependent upon your healing the three major issues that many human beings have: feeling unsafe, wanting power over others, and having a low sense of self-worth. These issues – which correspond to the first three chakras* – have their roots in erroneous beliefs. They threaten your ego and cause you to make unconscious choices that are not always in your highest good.

Your spiritual evolution can slow to a crawl when the needs of your ego and pride make you deaf to God's guidance and restrict your growth. When you uncover the hidden parts of yourself in your shadow, the choice is yours whether to change them or not. I guarantee you, the more you let go of your shadow and allow your soul to shine, the more you will be able to hear your guidance, and the less you will feel separate from God.

Ironically, feeling separate from God can actually prevent you from receiving guidance. It's like sitting in a house waiting for God to call back, but you don't have a telephone.

*   *   *

I did a reading for a Jan, a woman in her early

---

* There are seven major energy centers, or chakras, in the body. They are located near your spine and run from the top of your head (the "crown" chakra) to your tailbone (the "root" or first chakra). Each chakra correlates to specific physical and emotional energies.

sixties, who had spent her entire life feeling inferior to others. She came to see me because she was slightly depressed and felt a general malaise in regard to the world. I did a reading and found no significant physical problems. Her emotions were shut down, however, and her connection to God was completely cut off. Her crown chakra, which is the conduit for our connection to God was completely closed. She was receiving no inspiration or guidance and felt disconnected from the spiritual realm. This is a really difficult way to exist. It feels very lonely and can be quite frightening. There is an emptiness inside. It's like shrouding your soul in darkness.

The priority task for Jan was to open up her crown chakra and reconnect to her Higher Power. Without reconnection her soul would not thrive and she would continue to become more depressed, more desolate, and more

Gratitude

Please help me remember to be grateful for my gifts and talents, my guidance, and my ability to make choices that will improve my life. Being grateful raises my vibration while bringing me closer to God.

convinced that she was defective. She would drift away into an apathetic place where she would go through the motions of life without any real feeling, without any real passion, and without any real connection to God, to others, or to herself.

The quickest way to reconnect to God is to pray gratitude. I took Jan's hand so we could pray gratitude for all the wondrous things in her life. She looked at me as though I had two heads – her life sure didn't *feel* wondrous – but she took my hand anyway. I began to give thanks for Jan's health, for her ability to appreciate the joy and beauty in life, for the people she had in her life, and for the longevity of her life. I prayed gratitude for the incredible day that we were experiencing. I thanked God for Jan's ability to reach out for help, for her courage to come to me and try to resolve her problem, for her awareness that there was a problem, and for her willingness to do whatever was needed to heal her spiritual issue.

Shortly into our prayers, Jan began to weep as she started to let the love of God into her heart. Slowly she began to realize that she didn't have to do anything to deserve God's love, that it was hers by virtue of just being alive in that moment. Jan saw that she *was* worthy of God's love.

And in that moment, as I held her hand, Jan felt

the power, the majesty, and the love of God. She felt herself being surrounded by angels. She felt herself opening up and surrendering to a power higher than ourselves. In that moment, Jan received grace and it changed her life forever.

I gave her "homework" to pray gratitude daily, keep her heart open, and reconnect with God. The lines of communication had been reestablished. Now she was ready to pray for guidance.

And now she would get it.

CHAPTER 10

Removing the Biggest Hurdle
to Hearing Your Guidance

Aren't the stories in this book about the intervention of angels amazing? They are absolutely true. I invented none of them nor added details to dramatize them. I have told them just as I lived them. Now the big question: has reading these accounts of grace in action made you more open to letting go of your stinking thinking? I hope so, because I want you to drastically increase your ability to have angels and guidance in your life.

*   *   *

There are three key steps to having all the divine help you could possibly want.

First, pay attention to the basics:

- Open the lines of communication to God by

praying gratitude daily.

- Ask for help.
- Honestly want the help you are asking for.
- Don't set any conditions on what kind of help it must be.
- Listen (and watch) carefully for a response.
- Remember that the guidance you receive may come at a much higher vibration than your request, so it may be hard to recognize or accept at first.
- If you hear nothing, wait. Perhaps you are supposed to rest for a while.
- If you prayed for protection, know that angels are with you even if it doesn't seem like they are.
- Accept that not all lives can be saved, even by prayer.
- When you recognize that you have received guidance – whether it was through an event that occurred, a voice that spoke in your head, the intervention of a stranger, or a message in a dream – say thank you.

Second, overcome the biggest hurdle to hearing your guidance: those erroneous family and cultural beliefs that dictate how life works and what you can

– and more often cannot – do in it. I call them "tribal beliefs." In this chapter, I'll show you how to recognize and change them – quickly.

Third, take a compassionate look at the state of your ego, and heal your issues of low self-esteem and pride. In the next chapter, I'll explain how you can do that.

*   *   *

Tribal beliefs are rules about life taught to you by your family, teachers, and religious institutions. The people in these groups make up your "tribe."

Discernment

Please help me tell the difference between divine guidance and my own wishful thinking. Help me to know that I can feel God's love anytime I choose to let go of the illusion that I am unworthy.

The purpose of your tribe – indeed, the purpose of any tribe – is to protect you, educate you, and raise you to adulthood so that you can become a useful member of it. The purpose of tribal beliefs is to bind the group together through a common belief system.

This is not a bad thing per se. Unfortunately, many

tribal beliefs are misguided or just plain erroneous. Even this wouldn't necessarily be a big problem if you knew they were just beliefs. The trouble is, tribal beliefs get treated like facts. So you think they are facts.

Here are some tribal beliefs that you may think are facts:

- *Blood is thicker than water.*

- *There is no such thing as a free lunch.*

- *Anything worth having is worth working hard for.*

- *You heard some other tribal beliefs in Chapter 2 when I shared some of the reasons people have given me for not asking for guidance. Do you remember these examples of stinking thinking?*

- *My problems are small, and it's not right to ask for help when there are people worse off than me, people who really need the help.*

- *Asking for help means I'm weak.*

- *If I ask for help and get it, I will owe something, and I don't like the feeling of owing something.*

- *If I struggle through on my own, it builds character.*

Can you see how these are beliefs, not facts? If not, consider these truths:

Your receiving guidance does not deprive any-one else of it. God is never going to run out of time or energy to help us.

Asking for help usually means you are smart enough to know when you need it.

Guidance doesn't come with a price tag. When your angels help you, you don't owe them a thing (except to say thanks).

If you struggle through on your own, you'll get exhausted. If you doubt it, look up the definition of "struggle."

Most people want a spiritual connection or path, but they have complicated the process with too many tribal beliefs. These hidden rules chip away at your sense of safety in the world ("Don't make waves.") and your desire to live ("Always play it safe"). They also interfere tremendously with your guidance ("Only priests can talk to God").

Often, tribal beliefs have their origins in feelings of inadequacy or unworthiness that have been passed down through generations and are now like law within a family. There are also tribal beliefs that are based upon our cultural heritage, religion, and even geographical location. These beliefs not only feel like facts, they even evolve into cultural clichés such as "No pain, no gain," and "Suffering is noble."

Besides disguising themselves as facts, tribal beliefs maintain their power by harshly penalizing those who reject them. To challenge a tribal belief is tantamount to saying the tribe is wrong, and that is forbidden. I remember the character Ayla in Jean Auel's *Clan of the Cave Bear*. In Ayla's tribe women were forbidden to touch weapons. When she uses a weapon to save a child, she is deemed "dead" by the tribe, and they abandon her in the wilderness.

Do you think things have changed since then? Try telling your family or friends that you don't have to work hard to succeed. You'll see.

Tribal beliefs about the spiritual realm can be much subtler than the examples I gave you earlier. They come in the guise of religious instruction and it's a rare child who doesn't swallow them hook, line, and sinker. Here are some of the "facts" my clients were taught about angels.

Mary: "My tribe taught me that only spiritual people can communicate with angels. Spiritual people were not ordinary people like us, therefore angels were beyond our reach."

Natalie: "Angels are sacred, like saints, and should not be bothered for mundane, earthly matters. It would be almost sacrilegious to call for help from such a spiritual being."

Robert: "Angels only guard little children, and once you grow up you have to take care of yourself."

These "facts" are not only wrong, they stand in the way of receiving an enormous amount of help in the form of guidance, inspiration, comfort, and angelic intervention.

Often people refuse to let go of their tribal beliefs because it feels like being disloyal to their family. I've said it before and I'll say it again: tribal beliefs severely slow or limit your spiritual evolution. If you are not on a spiritual path or aren't interested in your purpose in life, then carry on as usual. You will evolve spiritually at the rate of your tribe. If you have ever tried to coordinate fourteen family members in picking a restaurant and meeting there at the same time for dinner, then you understand how a tribe operates and can imagine just how fast they evolve.

But if you can identify and let go of your tribal beliefs – about guidance and anything else – you will have cleared a huge hurdle in your spiritual path. And your life will change for the better immediately.

*　　　*　　　*

So how do you jettison the tribal beliefs that are limiting your spiritual growth and denying you joy? I'm going to show you exactly how to do it. First I'll explain the steps, then I'll use an example offered by one of my clients to show you what the process looks like in action.

There are seven steps to changing tribal beliefs.

1. Ask yourself if it's possible that a tribal belief is causing your distress.
Are you upset or frustrated by something or someone? Does your life seem too hard or unfair? Are you tired of _____ (fill in the blank)? At the root of your feelings may be an erroneous tribal belief. Many difficult and uncomfortable feelings are actually caused by tribal beliefs. If you need help seeing what it is, ask someone you trust. Often other people can spot our tribal beliefs more easily than we can.

2. Put it into words. Once you have uncovered a tribal belief, find exactly the right words to express it. Make sure the words are specific to you. You'll know you've hit pay dirt because it will click. When you write or speak it, you may even be able to feel it run through your body.

3. Decide whether the tribal belief is good for you or not.[*] Does it energize you or drain you? Does it raise your vibration or lower it? Does it contribute to your spiritual evolution or slow it down?

4. If the tribal belief is good for you, embrace it, and skip the rest of these steps. Live your belief

---

[*]Although I've focused here on negative tribal beliefs, there are some that are helpful. Keep reading.

as often as possible. For example, for some people the tribal belief that families should eat together is a high vibration belief. They enjoy these gatherings and feel a sense of love and unity. They should arrange to have meals together as often as possible.

5. If the tribal belief is not good for you, look at how it plays out. How does that belief manifest in your daily life? What does it look like? What choices and decisions are you making (or not making) that are based on it? You might also look at how that belief has played out in years past. I want you to really get how big an effect the tribal belief is having on your life.

6. Make a conscious choice to rewrite your tribal belief or let it go. Many people find that rewriting their belief is the most effective way to change it. If you do this, work on your rewrite until it really clicks. Ask yourself, "What would I rather believe instead?" Then spend some time and find exactly the right words, the ones that demolish the old tribal belief and state something you know is true. Don't fake it.

For example, a client once told me, "Only stupid people pray to God for help. Smart people help themselves." The result of this tribal belief was that she struggled constantly with her fears and her separation from God. So I tried to suggest something that would feel true to her without feeling overwhelming. I didn't try to get her to believe that asking for help was smart. That was too big a step. I simply asked her if it was reasonable to consider asking for help once in a while? She thought it over and said yes. Her new tribal belief is: "It is reasonable to ask God for help now and again." As time goes by and she grows spiritually, I expect she will revise this belief even more.

7. Write it down and practice it. After rewriting or letting go of the tribal belief, write your new belief in your Tribal Log, and say it out loud to yourself and others for two weeks. You'll be amazed at the results.

One of my clients has a gift for helping others. She was good at it and she enjoyed it. The problem was, she didn't include herself in the equation. Despite having work she "loved," she was depressed and tired all the time. The years were slipping by and joy wasn't even on her horizon. She felt something important was missing in her life, but she didn't know what it was.

I suggested she do some work on her tribal beliefs, and that she start with looking at beliefs about doing things for others. She agreed and used free association to come up with a list:

- *Helping others is good.*
- *Good people help others.*
- *People need help and I am good at helping them.*
- *People should do what they are good at.*
- *If you're good at something, that's what you should be doing.*
- *Doing what other people want is kind.*
- *Doing what I want is selfish.*

BINGO! That last belief really hit home. It felt right. Not that the other beliefs weren't true in her mind, but the last belief was the one at the heart of the matter. It was this belief that was driving her to help others to the exclusion of herself.

Her next step was to look at how the belief that doing what she wanted was selfish manifested in her life. That was easy. She gave me six or seven examples. Times when she had listened to friends for hours when she had other things she wanted to do. Times when she had worked so long on her client's projects that she didn't have the energy for her own hobbies and pleasure. Times when she gave in or pleased someone at her own expense.

"So, does this belief drain you or energize you?" I asked.

"It drains me," she replied without hesitation. "And I'm going to rewrite it."

"Okay, what will you choose to believe instead?"

Her new list of beliefs, which she also free-associated, went like this:

- *Doing what I want is my birthright.*
- *Other people can take are of themselves.*
- *I am not responsible for their lives or their feelings.*
- *I do not have to spend my time with people who lower my vibration, even if they are my mother.*
- *Doing what I want is the key to my survival.*
- *Doing what I want is being myself.*
- *Being myself is the greatest gift I can give.*
- *Being myself = doing what is right for me.*
- *Doing what I want is a gift to the world.*
- *Doing what I want is being authentic.*

Another BINGO! Being authentic was a very high personal value of hers, higher even than sharing her gifts with the world or setting limits with other people. When she came up with that belief, she knew she was home. She went out and bought a beautiful blank book to use as her Tribal Log, wrote down her first new belief, and remembered to say it out loud to herself and selected friends in the next several weeks.

People are skeptical when I tell them this process really works, that you can change the beliefs of a lifetime this easily. If you are one of them, I recommend exploring the tribal belief that says change has to be long and hard.

CHAPTER 11

'My Pride Has Toppled Me and I Can't Get Up'

You are on your spiritual path this very moment, while reading this book. By being present and staying open to a new way of thinking, you are expanding spiritually. You have started looking at your tribal beliefs so you can make better choices in your life. Whether your choice be to simply pray for the world each day, step out of a powerless victim state, or listen to the guidance that is shouting from the depths of your soul, you will be taking a huge step in your spiritual evolution. Congratulations!

*   *   *

Don't stop there. Don't let pride close your heart to God's help. Go a step further and own who you really are, a spiritual being in the process of learning and growing. Let go of your need to be right. Don't let pride stand in the way of your spiritual evolution. When you relax and allow God or your Higher Power to guide you, you can be of service to others and help heal the planet. Lord knows, it needs it.

The downfall of man is always caused by pride. This is true whether that downfall be one's health, relationship, finances, or professional success. Taken to its extreme, pride is the cause of blood feuds. It is the fuel for revenge, hatred, jealousy, suffering, and denial. It makes you loudly reject the suggestion that your tribal beliefs are stinking thinking.

Talking about pride is tricky. Some people have told me that pride means thinking too well of yourself or acknowledging your ability to play the piano skillfully. Pride is akin to boasting, they say.

Safety

Please help me feel safe and secure in my life by reminding me that help is always available to me and I am never alone.

I want you to think outside the box and consider a different way of looking at pride. Try this one: pride is the tendency to dig in your heels and refuse to know anything but what you already know. It's true.

And pride stands between you and God. That's why pride is responsible for your life being harder than it has to be.

Let me give you an example. I worked with a woman who has struggled most of her life. Nancy was a single parent with a high-stress job and few friends. She wasn't very happy. But suggesting to her that she could ask for help and her life could be easier was no easy task. She sputtered in anger that her life couldn't be easier because of her past "mistakes." She didn't really deserve an easier life. (You can probably recognize this by now as a tribal belief.)

Nancy needed to be right, so she clung to her convictions. However, the truth was, her life could be easier and her "mistakes" did not bar her from God's help. I gave her a few seconds to bask in her excuses, then said, "What if I tell you not only how you have contributed – quite generously – to your life being difficult, but why you won't consider changing it." That got her attention.

"You don't want an easy life. You wear your struggle like a badge of honor. You take great pride in your fortitude, your ability to keep going no matter the odds against you. You are proud of the way you persevere in the face of adversity. If I took that adversity away, you would feel like a nobody."

I have to give Nancy credit. She had the smarts

and good grace not to explode in angry defenses and rationalizations about her life. She looked me squarely in the eye and said, "You're right I won't ask anyone for help, not my family or God or spiritual guides. If life were easy…"

Her voice trailed off as she realized that deep down she was in a huge conflict. She hated struggling in life but was afraid if she didn't struggle and overcome, she would not only have no self-esteem but she wouldn't be able to be forgiven and pay for her "mistake": getting pregnant out of wedlock. Nancy's pride in punishing herself and living in struggle had become more important than anything else in her life.

Her pride in her agenda had blotted out God's love, and her stubbornness had contributed to a low vibration in her corner of the world. She dug in her heels, wore her struggles like a badge of honor, and ceased to grow spiritually or change any aspect of her life—even though

Serenity

God grant me the serenity to accept the things I cannot change, the courage to change the things I can, and the wisdom to know the difference.

she was clearly conscious of having a choice to live differently. Her low vibration eventually drove away all of the people in her life. Sadly, as she nears the twilight of her life, she still refuses to accept God's love or her inherent gifts and talents, and is still pay-ing dearly for her earlier "mistake." Her pride in being right has darkened her soul.

Pride

Please help me let go of my false humility and know that my abilities are a gift from God. Remind me to take care of myself so I can be of service to others.

One of my male clients told me he takes great pride in working hard for his family. Sounds good, doesn't it? The problem was, it was all about his agenda and needs. Let me give you some back-ground and a translation. John worked hard all the time – on workdays, days off, during his free time. He worked hard whether he felt good, bad, or downright sick. He worked when he was in pain. In fact, he worked even harder when he was in pain. He never took a day off.

John considered this honorable. He took pride in

the fact that he could keep working against all odds. The badge of honor John wore may have been invisible, but it was so huge, he actually walked tilted to one side.

If John's ability to persevere against all odds were taken away, he would consider himself a failure as a husband, father, and man. He attached his self-worth to his ability to struggle through adversity and wake up the next day to do it all over again.

What I saw was a man slavishly attached to his tribal beliefs, a man willing to die for his convictions. Sadly, John refused to consider that he was being prideful in an unhealthy way and worked himself into an early grave.

There is a strong reason why I say that pride is always the cause of a person's downfall. Holding on to your tribal beliefs can ruin your life. Because you cannot entertain other possibilities, you remain locked in your position. You are destined to keep wearing that exhausting badge of

---

✦

Integrity

Please help me be true to my spiritual nature, discern truth from illusion, and make choices that bring me closer to God.

---

honor. It is more important for you to be "right" than happy, healthy, or even alive.

Sometimes pride hides under the guise of humility. I worked with a woman named Ginger, who is quite a painter. Yet, when I remarked on her talent, she brushed me aside. "I'm okay," she replied. "There are others much better. Now da Vinci, he was a real painter." Ginger's need to be right in her assessment of her talents actually prevented her from rating them highly enough. Do you see how pride can lurk beneath false humility?

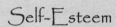

Self-Esteem

Please remind me to be grateful for my talents and abilities and not diminish or hide them, but rather show me how to share them easily with others.

Nancy, John, and Ginger are classic examples of people whose self-esteem comes from the outside, not the inside. All three of them could heal on many levels—especially their spirits, if they chose to give up their pride in being right.

When you have no self-esteem, you must garner praise and accolades from others to feel good about yourself. You are dependent on your boss's approval, a critic's opinions, your spouse's smile, and your friend's remarks. Unfortunately, even if you win such accolades, your self-esteem can be taken away the moment anyone says something critical. When one art critic said Ginger's painting was great, she had a short-lived high…until another critic said it stunk. She was like a tiny rag doll buffeted by the ever-changing winds.

CHAPTER 12

Lock and Load Your Self-Esteem

*As Marianne Williamson has so eloquently written:
"Our greatest fear is not that we are inadequate, but
that we are powerful beyond measure. It is our light, not
our darkness, that frightens us. We ask ourselves, Who
am I to be brilliant, gorgeous, handsome, talented and
fabulous? Actually, who are you not to be?*

*"You are a child of God. Your playing small does
not serve the world. There is nothing enlightened about
shrinking so that other people won't feel insecure
around you. We were born to make manifest the glory of
God within us. It is not just in some; it is in everyone.
And, as we let our own light shine, we consciously give
other people permission to do the same."**

---

* From Chapter 7 of *A Return to Love*

*   *   *

Acknowledging your gifts and talents fills you with a sense of self-esteem. It allows you to own your personal power and not give it away to others. When you have good self-esteem – which you develop by making commitments

Strength

Please help me be aware of my abilities and to call upon them when I doubt my strength to move forward in life.

to yourself that you keep, valuing your personal code of honor, owning your gifts and talents, and letting go of false humility – you do not look for attention or validation from others. If you know you are an ethical person and someone calls you unethical, you don't fall apart. Your strength is inside; you know your worth. The winds can blow until the cows come home, and it has no impact.

What's more, when you don't own your talents, such as painting well, being a good listener, being able to stay cool in an emergency, having a good sense of humor, or being a good friend, you are dishonoring God.

Think of it this way. When you fill out a resume,

do you neglect to mention your abilities or talents in your field? If you did, wouldn't it dishonor all the people who taught, mentored, or otherwise helped you learn and grow professionally over the years? Besides, what employer would want to hire you? Owning all of your talents – in every field – builds your self-esteem and frees you from being stuck in your pride. You can have true self-esteem instead of the false self-esteem that comes from things like basking in your ability to constantly overcome adversity and tough things out.

*   *   *

I have a client who I think is simply amazing. He is funny and warm, a bright light on the planet. Yet he has low self-esteem and little confidence or courage in certain areas. Put him in a business arena and he can outdo Donald Trump. But put him in a relationship, and his fire goes out. When I asked him to tell me why he was amazing, he was quite taken aback at first.

"I never thought of myself as amazing," he mused.

"Well, I do," I countered. "So out with it."

All he could find to say was that he had a good business mind, and perhaps that was mildly amazing.

I looked at him and tried a different approach.

"Tell me who you are, what qualities you have, how someone would describe you."

He said he was kind, compassionate, and funny.

"That's a great start," I said. "Now tell me what makes you who you are. What is it about you that you can always count on? For example, in times of stress are you the one who keeps his sense of humor and doesn't lose his cool?" I already knew this was true, but I waited for him to nod in agreement. "And are you a good listener to your friends?" He nodded again.

I felt like a dentist extracting teeth, but eventually I pulled a list of his qualities from him. He looked nonplussed as the list grew.

"How can you call being compassionate or being a good listener a talent or gift?" he protested. "We're supposed to be that way."

Here was a classic example of a hidden tribal belief being unveiled. I quickly scanned his energy and saw a picture of him sitting contentedly on his deck. I said, "How about Andrea Bocelli? Do you think he is a talented singer?"

"Oh, yes," he replied, "I love to listen to him when I'm out on my deck. He's marvelous, so very talented."

"So, singing is a talent or gift, but being a good listener or leader is not?"

"Well...yes."

My client considered singing as a gift from God because he couldn't do it. The value of his own gifts and talents was negated because they were his. This is false humility, even if he is not conscious of it being so. The point is, he is certain he is right: Andrea Bocelli is gifted and he is not. We're back at pride.

Many people believe it is boastful to acknowledge their gifts and talents. Their family has taught them never to blow their own horn. I can't tell you how many clients have this tribal belief. Are you ready for the truth about this one? The false modesty of ignoring or downplaying your gifts and talents is a slap in God's face. You received a gift, yet will not own it.

What's more, if you hide behind false modesty, you'll never acknowledge who you are, you'll never know what you are capable of, and you'll never develop the courage to get out in the world and try something new – start a relationship, go on a safari in Africa, get out of a bad marriage, or trust God when you are told to leave your job.

*   *   *

We want to hang on to what we know because it defines us. It feels safe and familiar. Tribal beliefs hold people together and there is a false security in those numbers. Standing alone takes courage. Looking for people with similar beliefs takes effort. Letting go of your pride in "knowing what is right" takes practice, and it requires you to tolerate the fear that may come up when you step into the unknown territory of "I don't know." But when we heal the part of us that feels unworthy, the part that doesn't value our own gifts and talents, all these things suddenly become easy.

Here are ten ways to assess and boost your current level of self-esteem. Put your answers in a log entitled "Who I Really Am." Refer to it often. I cannot emphasize enough how important this is to your spiritual evolution.

Find out who you are. Describe yourself on paper as if you were writing about a friend. Be honest and list at least five wonderful things about yourself.

Determine what qualities you have that you can always count on. Write down why you would choose yourself as a partner on a two-week expedition across the Canadian

---

Humility

Please help me let go of my need to be right, my arrogance, and my illusion of self-importance and remember that I am loved unconditionally.

Rockies. Do the same thing with a six-week assignment to work closely together in your profession. If you find a good reason to dread that six-week assignment with yourself, consider changing that behavior. You can always make the choice to do so.

Identify and own the positive things your friends, co-workers, and/or family say about you. If nothing comes to mind, ask them why they like you. For example, I heard this comment over and over in the E.R.: "Christel, I love working with you because you know your stuff, and no matter what happens – even if we get a busload of hemophiliacs who've been hit by a train and there's no clotting factor 8 in the hospital –you remain totally calm and get the job done. We feel safe working under you."

Examine how you speak about yourself to others. Do you say, "I can play the piano?" Or do you say, "I play the piano well," or "I play with great feeling"? Notice when you downplay your abilities, and see if a tribal belief may be responsible. If so, REWRITE IT!

Notice how you respond to compliments. Do you receive them with embarrassment? Do you protest or brush the comment aside? Next time, button your lip, make eye contact, take in the compliment, and say thank you. Then write the compliment down in your log.

Be aware of how you respond to genuinely constructive feedback. Do you feel deflated? Do you get defensive or start explaining or rationalizing your behavior? Do you give your power away to the other person? Or do you listen, choose to consider what's been said, and eventually get back to that person for clarification, agreement or disagreement? Next time, take a breath while you listen, and make an agreement with yourself to look honestly at the person's feedback. Write about the experience in your log.

Pat yourself on the back for your achievements. Do you notice the good you do or only the mistakes and failures? Think of two things you did during the day that were good for you, for someone else, or for the overall vibration of the planet. Put them in your log. If nothing comes to you, then simply say a prayer for yourself and one other person.

Respect who you are. If you don't, why? What could you do differently so you would respect yourself? Pick one part of you that you would like to change, then focus on it for two weeks. Use your log. Make the commitment, and you'll be amazed at the result.

Think about the commitments you make to yourself and others. Do you keep them? If not, figure out why you commit to things you don't really want to do in the first place, and learn to say, "No." When you commit only to things you really, really want to do, you will be very pleased at your success rate.

End your day with gratitude for your gifts and talents, your health, and the beauty of a single flower. Before falling asleep, remember three wondrous things in your day, and tell God how grateful you are for them.

Remember, when you downplay who you are, it does not serve anyone's highest good. Rewrite those tribal beliefs, fill yourself to the brim with self-esteem, and enjoy your life! How would you rather your gravestone read: "Here lies Mark, a hard worker who struggled to overcome adversity"; "Here lies Alice and she was right"; or "Here lies Tara, a wondrously compassionate woman who could admit when she was wrong and played a mean piano"?

CHAPTER 13

What if Your Life Purpose Is Just to Be Happy?

Nowadays, almost everyone I meet seems to be on a spiritual path or is searching for a purpose in life. It's become very popular. Unfortunately, many people have cluttered their search with religious baggage. For example, there are those who believe that walking a spiritual path involves struggle or sacrifice, being alone in the world, or seeing all the difficult times in life as spiritual lessons necessary for their souls' evolution. Yet the truth is, if you take responsibility for what you have created and make choices that are good for you, you don't need to learn so many tough lessons.

Some people search in exotic lands for a more spiritually evolved person to bestow wisdom upon them or reveal a grandiose, meaningful, or important purpose in their lives. Others seem to require adherence to ritu-

als like meditation or vegetarianism to be spiritual. And yet, 99% of the people I have asked could not answer these questions: What's your purpose in life? How do you know when you have reached your goal and become a spiritual person? And what happens then?

I have a proposal for you: What if your purpose in life is simply to be happy? And what if being happy is a spiritual way of life? When you are happy, your vibration is high, you hear God's voice, live in the flow, and have a positive impact on the world. Your happiness is easily spread to other people in your family, your community and around the world — could this be a meaningful purpose? Imagine the possibilities!

Are you not drawn to and feel better around happy people? What if you are the one who has the courage to break with tribal ways and do what brings you joy? What if you are the one who shows others that following guidance makes life easy, light and fun? Do you have any clue of the ripple effect you would have on the people you meet? Are you ready to accept a leadership role in healing our world by being a spiritual being with a tremendous purpose in life?

A man named Francis said it best many years ago:

"Where there is hatred, let me sow love...
where there is despair, hope
where there is darkness, light
and where there is sadness, joy."

Make a difference in this world by contributing a high vibration of happiness, love, forgiveness, truth and joy into our world. Living in a high vibration– being happy – is our true spiritual nature. It contributes immensely to the healing of the planet and brings us closer to God. Isn't that a spectacular calling?

*   *   *

Remember the reading I did for Jan, who had to open the lines of communication with God by praying gratitude before she was able to hear her guidance? Two days after our prayers together, she called me. She was both excited and scared. Her guidance had told her to quit her job and retire, something she hadn't planned to do for another four years. She was excited because she no longer enjoyed her job, but she was scared because she wasn't sure if she could make it financially on her pension.

Then something else hit her. What would she *do* with the rest of her life? She prayed for more guidance, but heard nothing else. I encouraged her to follow her initial guidance. Everything would work out ten times better than it was at the moment.

Jan chose to trust her guidance and retire from work. She told me, however, that she still had heard nothing regarding her next step. We prayed together, and I heard Jan's guidance very clearly. It was this: *"Relax and enjoy your life."*

Jan was perplexed. "What kind of guidance is that?" she asked.

"Very clear guidance," I responded.

"How am I supposed to relax and enjoy my life?" she asked.

"First, you retire. Next you figure out what makes you happy. Then you do it," I said with a grin. "You like to garden, you like to visit art galleries, you like to be with your family, and you would like to have a dog. It's really quite simple."

Jan insisted that her guidance could not be so easy. Following guidance had to be much harder.

"Do you want to go to Rwanda and clean toilets?" I inquired. "Will that guidance be hard enough for you to follow?"

She nodded. She couldn't understand how having a good time could be guidance. "It's supposed to be hard", Jan insisted.

I pointed out to Jan that she had a tribal belief that following guidance meant doing something difficult or unpleasant, something that would be a sacrifice of some sort or require to her to lose something, be alone in life, or suffer in some other way. If this was Jan's idea of guidance, no wonder she'd never prayed for guidance before.

"Why would God want you to struggle, suffer, or sacrifice things?" I asked her. "That makes no sense. God *loves* you."

I explained to Jan that it would be okay to simply sit back, relax, and enjoy her life. She didn't have to have some kind of grandiose purpose or do something supposedly productive in the world.

"When you enjoy your life, you raise your vibration. A person's high vibration has a ripple effect in the world. Your happiness will be contagious. Spreading joy is definitely a worthwhile purpose in life."

Then I reminded Jan of the philosophy we have at the Center for Spiritual Responsibility: heal yourself, raise your vibration, and have a positive impact upon the world. Allow your high vibration to inspire others to heal. Make a difference in the world by taking care of yourself, and thus be of service to God and others.

Jan felt between a rock and hard place. She wanted to make a difference in the world and absolutely be of service, but she was determined to make her life harder than it needed to be. She was convinced that her purpose in life could not be so easy as to simply be happy. Her purpose *had* to be more than that.

There was one more snag. Jan wanted her guidance to come with a step-by-step instruction book and a money-back guarantee that all would be well if she followed it. That's not always how guidance works. Sometimes you are simply given the first step. You take it, and then you have to trust.

Whenever you have difficulty trusting what your angels or your inner voice is telling you, remember

> ✦
>
> ## Flexibility
>
> Please help me let go of my rigid beliefs and teach me to see the gray between what appears to be either "black or white."

that each and every time you followed your guidance in the past, you came out ten times better than before. Not just a little better. *Ten times better.*

*   *   *

Rick, 49, came in for a reading because he was having trouble with his heart. What my reading revealed was that his problems were rooted in not following his guidance. In other words, he had chosen a path that his heart wasn't in. His physical heart problems were manifesting the problem that his emotional/spiritual heart was having with the path he was taking.

Rick, an intelligent and charming man, had put tremendous time and money into a program of buying property so he could become financially independent. Each time he hit a block, he only worked harder to stay on course. While he did achieve some measure of success, he yearned for more and continually said affirmations to help him achieve it. Unfortunately, those affirmations were not in alignment with the needs of his soul, so they did him no good.

Because he had invested so much time and money in the seminars, books, tapes, and personal coaching from this program, his pride would not allow him to accept my reading that this was the wrong path for him. He didn't want to hear that he would not achieve the level of success that he wanted and would not become financially independent. He staunchly defended his position – and was therefore unable to hear his guidance for himself.

His wife, Blanchefleur, was able to accept my reading more readily, and at my suggestion, she prayed for guidance. Since their finances were tight at the moment, she decided to ask for guidance on whether to sell a piece

---

✧

Trust

Please help me to be more trusting of my intuition, of the signs I receive, and of God's love for me.

---

of their real estate to raise some cash. Rick was against the sale. Their property was their security blanket, he pointed out. It was supposed to bring them income during lean times.

Because the couple were new to the idea of guidance and prayer, I told Blanchefleur that when she prayed, she should ask for a "New York sign" so there would be no mistaking the fact that she was receiving guidance. A "New York sign" is what I call something that stops you in your tracks and forces you to take notice. If you've read my book *Diary of a Medical Intuitive,* you know that I asked for a New York sign at a crucial point in my life – and there was no doubt that I got it. I was literally stopped in my tracks on a narrow path in the Andes. There's no mistaking a New York sign.

Blanchefleur asked for a seemingly impossible sign: if her property manager called and quit within two hours of her prayer, she would know it was a sign—she had just spoken to him that morning and he expressed his joy for his job and working for her.

A scant two hours after Blanchefleur prayed for guidance, their property manager called from Arizona to say he was resigning. Without him, maintaining their investment property would be a huge burden.

Within five days, Rick and Blanchefleur were on

their way to following their guidance. They continued to pray and learned that they were supposed to open a healing center in Hawaii. This had actually been a dream of theirs years ago, before they had become so invested in the financial-independence-through-real-estate path that detoured them.

Can it truly be that easy? Here's the e-mail I recently received from Blanchefleur: "My dream of living in Hawaii is almost realized and creating a holistic healing retreat center feels so right, I have to just pinch myself sometimes."

*   *   *

I did a reading for Ken, a 57-year-old man with lung cancer. On the deepest level, he knew he was dying, but consciously he chose to ignore this. He was working a full-time job. Ken's vibration was low, not only from the illness, but because he was disconnected from God, spiritually adrift.

Ken had been angry with God when he was diagnosed with cancer, but now he just felt resigned to his fate. He had no connection with God, and I was saddened by the emptiness I saw inside him. Ken did not have that much time left here on earth, and I knew that his transition would be gentler and easier if he could reconnect with God before he went. It was time for some spiritual guidance.

Ken and I prayed together for guidance. In my

mind's eye, I saw a picture of him with a big grin on his face driving to various truck stops and ordering all kinds of pie. I didn't understand the guidance, but I told Ken what I saw.

His eyes filled with tears as a broad smile spread across his face.

"How could you know," he began, "that my dream is to eat at truck stops around the country and find the best pie?" Ken was known by his family and friends as a connoisseur of pie, and he loved to share the great pie destinations he discovered. In fact, he had often thought of writing the ultimate pie book.

It was clear that Ken's guidance was to allow himself some joy. This may seem like a simple task, but for some people it's not. When you get this kind of guidance, it's God's way of saying, *"You are loved, you are important, you deserve joy, and I want you to be happy."*

That afternoon Ken opened himself to God and wept. He understood now that he was loved and would not die alone. He could fulfill his dream of going on the great American pie hunt.

Most people don't understand that being happy is a way of being of service to others. Ken's situation reminded me of Johnny Appleseed. Whereas Johnny spread apple trees throughout the world, Ken would spread his high vibration, his joy, his contagious laughter and happiness, and the knowledge that having a difficult illness does not mean you have to stop living. Ken would also spread the message that being of service can be fun – it can even involve eating apple pie.

When I pray with people, what I hear is their guidance. This is another word for what I call a person's priority task – the single most important thing they can do right now to heal, and something that, when accomplished, will untangle a myriad of other problems.

Who would have thought someone's priority task could be so much fun? But the truth is, I've listened to some great guidance while praying with others over the years. It included: *"Learn to cook,"* *"Go shopping,"* *"Quit your job,"* *"Leave your relationship,"* *"Move to Hawaii,"* and, of course, *"Eat pie!"*

CHAPTER 14

Meeting the Angel of Death

Is there really an angel of death? Yes there is. But it's not a grim-reaper type of being who enters your room and takes you away when he decides it's your time to go. The angel – or multitude of angels – who come to accompany you at death are loving and reassuring.

*   *   *

That's because there truly is light – not darkness at the end of the tunnel. Each time I have crossed over with someone who has died, a slew of bright angels meets us on the other side. It's like coming out of a dark cave into an enormous room filled with the softest and most inviting light.

Anyone who has had a near death experience knows about this "room." Even though it is infinitely big, it still feels too small to hold all the love, light,

compassion, kindness, and joy that are in it. When
people cross over and see that room filled with angels, they remember who they really are: a part of
God. All illusions fall away and all earthly matters
become unimportant as they stand in wondrous awe
of God.

I am not allowed to enter this room. I can only
stand on the threshold and look in. Frankly, I'm not
sure my human brain could handle and process the
magnificence on the other side. I get just a glimpse, a
hint, a taste – something I experience with all my
senses – before being sent back.

One minute I am with the person who has died
and the next they have gone into the room and I am
standing alone. The light begins to recede, and I feel
like I am being sucked backward to earth. I always
return with the paradoxical feeling of being happy
the person has died – I have seen the joyful place
where he has gone. Later, as my impressions of that
wondrous room begin to dim, I am awash in sadness
over losing them.

I feel so privileged to even briefly get to see the
ethereal bliss we experience at death. To say it is
"life-changing" is an understatement. "Extraordi-
nary" doesn't come close. Experiencing my spirit un-
fettered by my body, is so uplifting and so ecstatic, I
find it almost painful to return. I know that when

people die their new lives are so filled with this unconditional love, that it heals their pain of leaving us behind. Can you imagine tasting that unconditional love here on earth? You can. All of us can. This book has shown you how. Start with praying gratitude, then open your heart to God and ask for guidance.

Protection

Please help me heal my body and mind with rest and revive my spirit by listening to my guidance. Teach me to let go of doubt and ask for the angels' help.

*   *   *

My experiences in the E.R. have shown me that no one is alone when they die. When death is imminent, an angel hovers in your room. I've seen both clusters of angels and a solitary angel waiting to accompany someone. (More angels are not better than one angel; the number of angels does not change the amount of comfort or peace you feel.) Sometimes the light from these angels is very soft and other times extremely bright. I believe the amount of light around someone who is about to die is directly proportional to the person's need. In the bedrooms and hospital rooms of people who have accepted their impending death, are at peace, and are ready to embrace God, I have seen one angel hovering quietly in the corner. People who die traumatically or suddenly, usually have a crowd of angels around them. When I am with people who have fought to the bitter end to hang on to life, I see the brightest light of all. I think all that light helps them find their way back to God. In short, people who are scared to die need a lot of light, a lot of angels. People who trust in the afterlife do not.

Yet even with angels lighting your way, you still have choices when you die. It is always your choice whether or not to enter that room filled with angels. Sometimes people linger outside it for a day – or for years. Pride can even hurt us in the afterlife. These lost souls need all our prayers in order to step over the threshold.

Last year I took my friend Teri to the doorway of the afterlife to show her what awaited her. She was dying of breast cancer that had spread to her liver, bones, and brain. When I entered her hospital room, there were angels sitting with her. It's hard to explain how comforted I felt, even though my dear friend was dying.

Although Teri could feel the angels' presence, she – like most people – didn't want to leave this earth. Part of her was thinking about her family and friends, and a small part of her was worried about the afterlife. She believed in God and the afterlife, but she was also a little scared that maybe it was all a hoax made up to make us feel better.

I took her hand and quietly brought her spirit to the place between heaven and earth where angels reside as they watch over us. Immediately her pain-induced agitation lessened. Her breathing slowed and became even. A beatific look spread over her face. Her jerking seizure movements stilled as she drank in the light and love of those angels.

It is impossible to be in that place and maintain our earthly qualities, like fear. The joy is immense, almost too much for our hearts to capture. Each time I go there I don't want to return to earth. It is light while earth is darkness. It is joy rather than pain, love rather than hate, and a feeling of connection with so many other lives rather than isolation. It is the ultimate feeling of belonging.

Taking someone you love to the afterlife is both devastating and wonderful. My earthly self is sad but my divine self is ecstatic. Having sure knowledge of the beauty of the afterlife kept me sane when patients in the E.R. – especially children – didn't make it and when my friend Teri died. There were many times my earthly self wanted to protest the seeming injustice of a life taken too early. But for the person who dies, it's not that way. Their firsthand knowledge of the existence of God and that room full of angels erases all their memories of the pain, betrayal, and loss they suffered here on earth.

Teri's face after her preview of the afterlife silenced my protests to God about the injustice of her early death. She looked at me with such love. "Thank you, from the bottom of my heart," she said. Even though she was ghastly ill, a light emanated from her that gave us both peace. When I left her, she was serene.

*   *   *

Before I learned how to cross over with people, I had two glimpses of what awaits us after our death. The first was when my grandmother died, and the second was in the E.R.

I was a proud new RN when my grandmother contracted terminal cancer. The illness brought her intense pain, wasted away her body, and eventually caused her to pray for a quick death. My grandmother endured her suffering quietly. She taught me that there is a hero in each of us, even when we feel afraid. To the end, she kept her sense of humor. At times she even became the comforter, not the one comforted. I prayed daily for her easy passage.

I had stayed with my grandmother that night

because I felt she was going to die, and I had the absurd notion that she might die alone. Sitting at her bedside, I watched the release of her spirit as she drifted into a coma, ready to leave. I prayed for an angel to come to her when she passed. Suddenly my grandmother sat bolt upright, eyes wide and gazing directly into mine. My breath caught in my throat as the light in her eyes illuminated the room, my soul, and my heart. I felt joy unlike any other, and I wept tears of gratitude for the ecstasy she was clearly feeling. When the light in her eyes slowly dimmed, I whispered, "I love you." I felt wrenched from something my soul needed, but there was nothing I could do: the light was receding. Slowly she collapsed in my arms, smiling, at peace, and looking years younger.

Three years later, working in the E.R., I felt like I was watching my grandmother die all over again. My patient's name was Mrs. Alston. She and my grandmother looked nothing alike, but cancer seemed to hit them the same way: the pain, the wasting body, and the desire for it to be over. Mrs. Alston's way of handling her illness was the same, too. She shielded her family from her agony, refused painkillers so she would be lucid enough to say goodbye, and fought to hang on long enough to see her son one last time, just as my grandmother had hung on to see my uncle.

I prayed for an angel to meet Mrs. Alston at death. Her time was nearing when her son finally arrived. So much was said in the simple and devoted look that passed between them. Mrs. Alston's spirit began to release quite peacefully. Suddenly she sat bolt upright and stared straight ahead for several seconds with a look of pure ecstasy. The light from her eyes was blinding. Then she took her last breath.

I could not yet fathom what my grandmother and Mrs. Alston had seen, but I knew I wanted to see the same thing when my time came.

I now know that I will. And so will you.

Guidance 24/7

Read an Excerpt From
Diary of a Medical Intuitive

Shortly after I started working in the E.R., a young teenager came in feeling unwell…The doctor examined him and didn't see anything wrong. "You're probably just working out too much," he told the young man. "But let's be sure. We'll draw some blood and do a urine sample." I gave the boy a few minutes alone, then went back and took the little cup he handed me. As I left the examining room, I looked down and saw that his urine had a green hue. I hurried to the doctor and showed him the urine sample. He looked at me with a slight frown.

"It's so awful he has leukemia," I said with compassion. I assumed the doctor, too, had seen what struck me as an unmistakable sign of the disease. The doctor, however, had seen nothing of the sort. He thought I was nuts – until the lab results came back showing the markers for leukemia. Then he thought I was scary. Although this kind of sudden "knowing" happened more and more in my work as a nurse, it didn't put a dent in my obstinate denial that I was an intuitive. After all, there was no such thing.

The more I doubted the veracity of my gift, however, the stronger the evidence for it became. No matter how hard I worked at ignoring or finding logical explanations for what I was experiencing, one thing became perfectly clear. Before the lab tests were run, I knew my patient's diagnosis….

Give the Gift of Healing

For additional copies of *Guidance 24/7*, or to buy **Christel's popular first book, *Diary of a Medical Intuitive*,** go to your favorite local bookstore. You may also call us at (760) 632-8780, or order the books at www.christelnani.com.

To request that your book(s) be signed by Christel, tell us when you call or email us (info@christelnani.com) and reference your online order.

Christel also has three wonderful CDs, which can be found at www.christelnani.com or www.amazon.com.

- **SPIRITUALITY, PRAYER & GUIDANCE:** Eliminate the misconceptions and conflicts that stand between you and God. Learn how to find your own spiritual path.

- **HEALING THE FIRST THREE CHAKRAS –** The chakras make up the mind-body connection and reveal much about your life. They are highly sensitive barometers of health that become ill before your body does. This CD explains the ways in which your thinking and fears affect your vital first three chakras, and it shows how to heal them.

- **DIARY OF A MEDICAL INTUITIVE** – Explains the concept of energetic illness and tells an amazing story of what can happen when you follow the guidance that is there for you. Also introduces the listener to the damaging power of tribal beliefs and shows how to determine if these beliefs are energy enhancing or energy depleting.

You can learn more from Christel...

Christel's CDs are available at Amazon.com, or ChristelNani.com.

- *Archetypal Transformation: Healing the Big Four Within You: Child-Saboteur-Victim-Prostitute.* Learn how to make your archetypes work for you!

- *Spirituality, Prayer & Guidance:* Eliminate the misconceptions and conflicts that stand between you and God. Learn how to find your own spiritual path.

- *Healing Your First Three Chakras:* The chakras are sensitive barometers of health that become ill before your body does. This CD explains the ways in which your thinking and fears affect your vital first three chakras, and how to heal them.

- *Diary of a Medical Intuitive: The Talk That Inspired the Book!* This riveting sold-out presentation includes stories of Christel's clairvoyant gifts, her discoveries of how the human energy system works, and her experiences of escorting people to the other side when they die that leave no doubt in the listener's mind about the powerful and loving presence of God.